D0066351

Getting the Most Out of Your Interactive Whiteboard: A Practical Guide

Amy Buttner

EYE ON EDUCATION
6 DEPOT WAY WEST, SUITE 106
LARCHMONT, NY 10538
(914) 833–0551
(914) 833–0761 fax
www.eyeoneducation.com

A sincere effort has been made to supply the identity of those who have created specific strategies. Any omissions have been unintentional.

Figures 1.1, 1.3, and 1.12 are reproduced with the permission of SMART Technologies.

Copyright © 2011 Eye On Education, Inc. All Rights Reserved.

For information about permission to reproduce selections from this book, write: Eye On Education, Permissions Dept., Suite 106, 6 Depot Way West, Larchmont, NY 10538.

Library of Congress Cataloging-in-Publication Data

Buttner, Amy.
  Getting the most out of your interactive whiteboard : a practical guide /
Amy Buttner.
     p. cm.
  Includes bibliographical references.
  ISBN 978-1-59667-169-0
  1. Teaching—Aids and devices. 2. Interactive whiteboards. 3. Education-
al technology. I. Title.
  LB1044.88.B88 2010
  371.33′5—dc22
                                                                2010035865

10 9 8 7 6 5 4 3 2 1

Also Available from EYE ON EDUCATION

Activities, Games, and Assessment Strategies for the Foreign Language Classroom
Amy Buttner

Differentiated Instruction Using Technology: A Guide for Middle and High School Teachers
Amy Benjamin

Organization Made Easy! Tools for Today's Teachers
Frank Buck

Rigor is NOT a Four-Letter Word
Barbara R. Blackburn

Critical Thinking and Formative Assessments: Increasing the Rigor in Your Classroom
Betsy Moore and Todd Stanley

How the Best Teachers Differentiate Instruction
Elizabeth Breaux and Monique Boutte Magee

Differentiating by Readiness: Strategies and Lesson Plans for Tiered Instruction, Grades K-8
Joni Turville, Linda Allen, and LeAnn Nickelsen

CALLing All Foreign Language Teachers: Computer-Assisted Language Learning in the Classroom
Tony Erben and Iona Sarieva

What Do You Say When…? Best Practice Language for Improving Student Behavior
Hal Holloman and Peggy H. Yates

How the Best Teachers Avoid the 20 Most Common Teaching Mistakes
Elizabeth Breaux

What Great Teachers Do *Differently*: 14 Things That Matter Most
Todd Whitaker

*This book is dedicated to
my husband Tim and my son Garrett*

Acknowledgments

I would like to express my sincere gratitude to the following people:

- Bob Sickles, for continuing to believe in my work and offering me the opportunity to develop this book.

- The Hartland-Lakeside School District and Therese Jilek, for the access to technology resources they have made available to my students and for the opportunities I have been provided to grow as an educator and share what I have learned with students and staff.

- Tim Zimmer, for his understanding and support during the book writing process.

- Kristen Anglemyer, for reviewing the manuscript and offering valuable feedback.

- Karen Brailsford, SMART Technologies Training Specialist, for her detailed technical support.

- My former teachers, who invested countless hours teaching me how to write.

- My students, for what I have learned from them has made me a better teacher.

Meet the Author

Amy Buttner is a Spanish teacher at North Shore Middle School in Hartland, Wisconsin. She graduated summa cum laude from the University of Wisconsin–Milwaukee with a major in Spanish and a minor in English as a Second Language. In 2003, she received her master's degree in history from the University of Wisconsin–Eau Claire.

Ms. Buttner has taught Spanish at the elementary, middle, and high school levels, and is a member of the Wisconsin Association of Foreign Language Teachers. She believes in the importance of global experiences for her students and has taken high school students to Argentina and middle school students to Costa Rica.

Ms. Buttner is dedicated to continued professional development. She has been working on effective integration of technology in the language classroom to promote and support language development. A particular area of research for the past three years has been effective use of the SMART Board in the classroom. During that time, she has become a SMART Certified Trainer, has conducted training sessions for teachers, and has presented on SMART Board use at Wisconsin Association of Foreign Language Teacher conferences. She has also developed and self-published SMART Board lessons for Spanish and English teachers.

Free Downloads

An overview of activities, tools, and ideas for using your interactive whiteboard is available on Eye On Education's website. Permission has been granted to purchasers of this book to download and print this overview. You can access these downloads by visiting Eye On Education's website: www.eyeoneducation.com. Click on the **Free** section, or search or browse our website to find this book's page.

You'll need your bookbuyer access code: **IWB-7169–0**

Bonus: A collection of more than 100 useful web resources that appear in the book can be found on our website. They are grouped by purpose and include the URL for each resource and a description of what you'll find there.

Contents

Introduction

Purpose of the Book

Most of our students come to school from media-rich, digital, interactive environments. To these students, learning is dynamic and information presented to them in a static way does not do much to excite them about learning. When used well, the interactive whiteboard is a tool that can engage our 21st-century students in learning on many levels.

The intention of this book is to be a practical resource that provides teachers with effective ways to use an interactive whiteboard in their classroom to improve student learning. The book is designed in such a way as to allow teachers to start using the interactive whiteboard immediately, building their skills and confidence, one step at a time. The book provides the following:

- ◆ Practical and realistic ways to start using the board immediately using existing media-rich and interactive resources.

- ◆ Ideas on how to start designing your own activities and lessons using the tools in the SMART Notebook software.

- ◆ Ideas on how to use the board as a tool for assessment in your classroom.

- ◆ Suggestions on how to get students creating and producing their own work using the board as a tool to share their work with an audience.

Value of the Interactive Whiteboard in the Classroom

As with any technology, there are skeptics who will question the cost-to-benefit value of technological products, as any good consumer should. When interactive whiteboards are used well, they are very much worth their cost. However, for teachers who are provided a board but no quality training, who lack interest in learning the tool, or who generally do not have effective instructional strategies, the interactive whiteboard runs the risk of becoming nothing more than a glorified dry erase board. The interactive whiteboard is, indeed, a powerful instructional tool, but it is important that teachers combine their quality instructional practices with effective training, resources, and support so they can tap into the potential of the board to positively impact and improve student learning.

The following are a few ways that students and teachers can use the interactive whiteboard to make the learning process more engaging.

- ♦ To pose questions, record discussions, and share results among classes.

- ♦ To learn about and evaluate information and concepts through multimedia resources (text, images, sound files, video clips).

- ♦ To access, discover, save, analyze, compare, discuss and evaluate information from a multiplicity of sources on the Internet.

- ♦ To practice key skills in an interactive way using

  - • existing activities, simulations, and games online.

  - • existing interactive resources that come with the interactive whiteboard software and through lesson materials, activities and games created by the teacher with resources in the software and online.

- ♦ To present key information and model important skills and processes.

- ♦ To examine, evaluate and discuss models of other student work and then apply what they have observed to their own work.

- ♦ To demonstrate and showcase student learning using a tool or tools of their choice to an audience of classmates or a global one.

Effectively using the interactive whiteboard in the above ways can:

- ♦ Increase students' level of interest and engagement in learning activities when lessons are more visually appealing.

- ♦ Improve student understanding of lesson material when they can physically interact with the lesson content by moving text and objects on the board.

- ♦ Improve student understanding of a lesson when they can intellectually interact with the content of the lesson, by causing students to view things in different ways and challenging why they think the way they do about certain topics.

- ♦ Increase student understanding of difficult, complex, and abstract ideas and processes through visual aids, interactive tools,

Flash files, video representations, and demonstrations of complicated processes.

♦ Help teachers formatively assess student progress through a multitude of practice activities.

♦ Provide students with more opportunities to be involved in leading lesson activities while the teacher guides from another place in the classroom as needed. This also allows the teacher to attend to student responses and engage in more formative assessment of students' understanding of the material.

Getting the type of results identified above can only happen when a teacher knows their content and knows how to design and implement quality lessons. It is also requires that the teacher dedicate time to learning how to effectively use the interactive whiteboard.

A Note to the Teacher

Without a doubt there is much to learn when you first start using an interactive whiteboard. Remember to take into consideration that whenever you learn a new skill, there is a new learning curve. Think about previous skills you have learned and the process involved in mastering them to keep perspective and be patient with yourself. Having learned most of what I know about the interactive whiteboard from exploration and trial and error, I am fully aware there are highs and lows when learning how to best use the board. I am also continually learning about what is best practice for using the interactive whiteboard through research and reflection on different instructional ideas I have implemented in my classroom. Be patient; keep trying new things that meet your learning objectives and engage your students, and honestly reflect on your teaching with the board. Before you know it, you will find that you have developed a substantial skill set that will help you improve student learning in your classroom. Learn from others as well; seek out other teachers in your district who use the interactive whiteboard, join communities of interactive whiteboard users online, and take useful tips students and colleagues give you about using the board. Also, make sure to take the time to celebrate your small successes along the way.

This book offers many ideas on how to use the interactive whiteboard in your classroom. These ideas can be used with any type of interactive whiteboard including Promethean, Mimio, Interwrite, SMART, and Hitachi boards, as well as others. However, when it comes to the specifics of using the software that accompanies the interactive whiteboard, this book provides explanations that refer to SMART Notebook Version 10.6. To get the most out of the book, you may find that it is beneficial to have a computer with SMART Notebook Version 10.6 installed and open for practice. You may also find it helpful to be near your interactive whiteboard for the beginning explanations. This book is primarily intended for individuals operating the SMART Board and SMART Notebook from a PC. However, there are very minimal differences between operating the software on a PC and on a Macintosh. If you are using a Macintosh, see the resource section at the end of the book entitled *Web Resources for Using Notebook 10 with a Macintosh* for helpful links to additional information you might want to reference.

1

Question and Explore

Getting Started

This chapter gives you ideas on how to get started with a whiteboard, whether you just found out you are getting an interactive whiteboard next week and are feeling frantic, or you've had one for awhile but need some ideas on how to start using it more.

Before beginning make sure that you have had some basic assistance from your technical staff. Ensure that the projector, computer, and SMART Board are properly hooked up and that you know how to turn on the projector, where to find the software on your computer, and how to open the software. You also need to know how to orient the board so it reacts correctly to your touch and how to clean the board to avoid damaging its electronic components.

Cleaning the Interactive Whiteboard

You will want to clean your interactive whiteboard surface as it starts to show fingerprint marks or become dirty. SMART Technologies recommends that for its interactive whiteboards you clean the writing surface or screen with a glass cleaner like Windex. You will want to spray the Windex on a soft cloth and then wipe the board. Spraying the cleaner directly on the board itself may result in damage to the electronic components of the board if, for example, the cleaner drips into the pen tray.

Orienting the Board

If you find that when you are writing on the board, the digital ink from your pen does not show up on the spot you are writing, you will need to re-orient the board. Interactive whiteboards that are mounted on a wall tend to need less frequent orientation than mobile versions. There are various places you can access the orientation function for a SMART Board, one of which is from the board's pen tray (Figure 1.1, page 4).

Figure 1.1. Pen Tray for Orienting

 OR

You will notice two buttons in the center of the pen tray—one with a keyboard icon and another with a mouse icon. Hold down both together for a couple seconds and you will notice that the orientation screen will pop up on your interactive whiteboard. Starting in the upper left-hand corner, touch the center of the plus icon (Figure 1.2) with your finger or a pen from the pen tray of the interactive whiteboard and then remove pressure. Move down each column moving from left to right repeating the action. When you touch the last plus icon in the lower right-hand corner, the orientation screen will disappear and return you to the original screen you were viewing. As you become more comfortable with the software you will discover that there are multiple locations from which you can orient the board. Use the one that is most convenient for you.

Figure 1.2. Orienting the Board

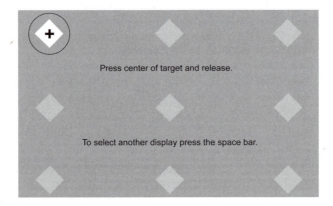

Keep Your Lesson Objectives in Mind

Before you begin to look for any resource or start thinking about what you want to do with the board and its software, make sure that you have a clear idea about what the purpose of your lesson is. It is easy to get caught up in the technology and lose sight of the purpose when you start learning the new tool and searching for lesson resources. The questions I always ask myself are: What is my lesson objective and what is the best tool to accomplish it with the resources I currently have available? Sometimes the answer to those questions do not involve a technology tool, which is okay as pencils and paper can be effective tools. However, you will likely find that the interactive whiteboard is a powerful tool that can be used for many learning purposes, both by itself and in conjunction with other learning tools.

Idea 1: Pose a Question

A great place to start using your board is with a good question or a problem for students to solve. You have likely discussed Bloom's Taxonomy and Higher Order Thinking Skills in a course or seminar during your educational career. A link to an updated digital version of Bloom's Taxonomy is listed in the Web Resources section of the book if you would like to review ideas on how to ask questions that promote higher order thinking. A valuable and effective use of the board may be as simple as posing a good question to get students to think and inquire about your lesson objective. A good question can lead to deep-level discussion, interaction and inquiry. To write a question on the board, you have two options.

Writing and Typing Text

The first option uses a pen. With the interactive whiteboard software open, walk to the board and pick up a pen from the pen tray (Figure 1.3). The pens use what is called digital ink. By pressing the pen with some pressure on the surface of the board and beginning to write, the top layer of the board connects with an inner layer and the digital ink appears when using a SMART Board. (Different interactive whiteboards use different methods for producing the writing.) If you do not have enough pressure, the ink will not appear. Write the question you would like to the students to see. Should you make a mistake, pick up the eraser from the pen tray and erase over the digital ink you would like to disappear applying light pressure.

Figure 1.3 Pen Tray

The second option does not require the use of a pen and the board to create the question. Using your computer and your mouse, click on the text icon represented in the main toolbar by an A with a red line underneath it. Multiple default text options will appear in a new menu. It is best to select one of the larger fonts by clicking on it with your mouse. Then click on the white workspace in Notebook and a text box will appear. In the text box, you can change features like font style, size, and color. Make any changes to the font before you begin to type where the cursor is. You can also select all of the information after you type it in the text box by highlighting it and apply any changes you need to make to the font. Once you have typed your question in the text box, click on the Select icon (represented by a black arrow) in the main toolbar. If you click on the workspace, your next click will give you a new text box.

Taking Notes and Adding More Pages

Depending upon the age level of the students that you teach, write or ask a student to write notes about the discussion that results from the question you pose while it is occurring. Doing so will provide a valuable record of students' thoughts that can be saved, shared among different classes, and printed for students. By looking in the main toolbar and clicking on the New Page icon (Figure 1.4) identified by a white piece of paper and a green circle with a plus sign, you can add a new page to your file to use for the notes. You or a student can also type the notes using the computer keyboard so they appear on the board if it is more efficient.

Figure 1.4. Add New Page

Add new page

Organizing Class Notes by Color or Groups

If you have more than one class and you want all of the notes from the day in the same file, you can color-code the notes for each class by using a different pen color for each set of class notes. Another way to keep separate notes from different classes that are organized in the same file is to create a group for each class. It is best to create the groups ahead of time for ease of organization.

To create new groups, click on the Groups button (Figure 1.5) and from the drop-down menu, select Edit Groups. On the new page that appears, click on Add New Group. Add as many groups as you would like by following the same procedure. Once you have as many groups as you want, you can label the group names. In the example, class periods are used. One way to relabel the groups is by double-clicking on the text "Group 1," etc. Double-clicking enables you to edit the text and relabel it.

Figure 1.5. Groups

Another way is to use the drop-down menu identified by the downward-facing triangle at the end of the blue title bar (Figure 1.6). Clicking on the triangle icon produces a drop-down menu that gives you options to delete, move, or rename the group. Selecting rename activates the text box the same way that double-clicking does. To exit the Edit Groups area, click on the red X in the upper right-hand corner of the screen or double-click on a page in any of the groups. You can also move individual pages in the Groups area. To move, click on a page and drag it to where you would like it to go. The same principle works with pages when you are no longer in the Groups area.

Figure 1.6. Editing Groups

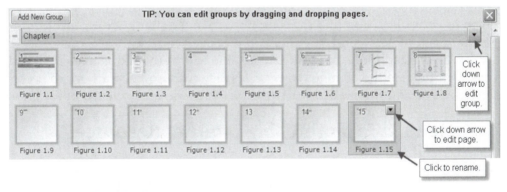

Saving and Printing

At the end of your discussion or lesson, you can save the file for future reference. You can save a Notebook file using the same process that you use to save most documents. From the File menu, you can select Save or Save As. There is also a Save icon in the main toolbar. A benefit of saving the notes from class, whether they be notes you create before or during class, is that you can also print them for any student who needs them. Before printing, it is a good idea to make sure the page background is white. To print from Notebook, go to the File menu and select Print. You will be given various options as to how you would like to print the Notebook pages, as well as what pages you want to print. You can also select whether or not you want to print the pages in landscape format.

Times When You Will Not Want to Save

There will be times when you will not want to save the changes you made to your lesson or you will want to save the file with a new name to maintain the original lesson without changes. You may have found a lesson from another source or have created one of your own and already understand why. Because of the interactive nature of the software that goes with the interactive whiteboard, you will be moving text and objects to interact with the lesson and reveal information. The next time you open the lesson you will not want to have to move everything back to its original location before using it. In this case, you can use the blue Undo icon in the main toolbar to undo changes you have made to the lesson. A second option is when closing the file, not to save any changes. This goes against the normal logic of when we work in programs like word processing, as we usually want the most recent version saved, so you may need to watch out the first few times you close an interactive whiteboard file. Another way to avoid saving changes to a lesson when you do not want to is to mark the file as "Read-Only." For SMART Notebook files, if you right-click on the file before opening it you can select Properties. From there, look for the section entitled Attributes. Click on the box to select Read-Only, which will prevent any changes from being made or saved to your file. If you find that you need to make changes to your file after you have made it a Read-Only file, you just need to repeat the same process and deselect Read-Only and you will be able to edit the file as usual. Should you want to keep the changes to your lesson, but also keep an original version of it, you can choose Save as from the File menu and give it a new name.

Idea 2: Explore Using Internet Resources

Accessing the Internet

Once you have posed a good question and your discussion begins, students may come up with more questions than answers. Being flexible in your lesson may lead you and the students to do some exploration for more information on the Internet. Because the interactive whiteboard is an enormous touch screen, you can open the Internet browser directly from the board by using your finger as the mouse and pushing down on the icon for the Internet browser you would like to open. You may have some information databases that your school subscribes to where you would like to start your search already bookmarked or in your toolbar. If so, click on the resources as you would at your computer, using your finger as the mouse. Many students instinctually seem to go straight to Google to search for information. If you are looking for a resource that will provide directed practices that teach students how to find, evaluate, and cite online information, you may want to take a look at the resources available on the CyberSmart website: http://cybersmartcurriculum.org/researchinfo/lessons/. If you could use a refresher yourself, try this PDF handout from Melissa S. Barker: http://whitepapers.virtualprivatelibrary.net/SearchTips.pdf

Using the On-Screen Keyboard

If you would like to do a search on the Internet using your search engine of choice, you will find a button with a keyboard icon on it on your pen tray. Pushing the button will open the On-Screen Keyboard (Figure 1.7). Make sure to select the address bar of the Internet where you would like to type in the website address by touching it with your finger. Begin typing letter by letter on the On-Screen Keyboard. Once you have finished typing, select Enter on the keyboard. You can also accomplish the same task by going to your computer keyboard if that is more efficient for you.

Figure 1.7. On-Screen Keyboard

Interacting with Internet Resources

Shortcuts to Maximize and Minimize Text Size

Once you find a resource of interest, there are some helpful tips and tools to interact with the information and help keep students focused on the information. Most times it is difficult to see the text on a web page when projected for an entire class. Using a shortcut can help you maximize the text size. Using the On-Screen Keyboard, touch the Ctrl button and then the = button. Do not hold them at the same time as you can only touch one spot on the interactive whiteboard at a time. Touching these buttons increases the size of the text on the page. Repeat the process until the text size is what you would like it to be. The same action will work from your computer keyboard, except that you will need to hold down the Ctrl button while pushing the + on the keyboard as many times as is needed to get the text the size you would like it to be. (The Cmd button on a Macintosh computer does the same thing as the Ctrl button on a PC.) To return the text on the website to its regular size, touch the Ctrl button and then touch the - button on your On-Screen Keyboard. Repeat the process until you have the desired size.

Focusing in

Using the Spotlight Tool

While you are examining an Internet resource, you may want to focus students' attention on a particular area or feature of the page. One tool you can use to do so is the Spotlight. SMART Notebook software includes a Floating Tools toolbar (Figure 1.8). When it is active, you will notice it "floating" on the side of your computer screen.

Figure 1.8. Floating Tools Toolbar

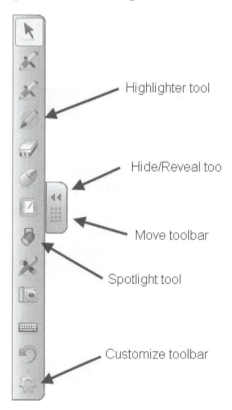

Highlighter tool

Hide/Reveal too

Move toolbar

Spotlight tool

Customize toolbar

Touching or clicking on the Hide/Reveal icon (represented by the double-arrow icon) on the Floating Tools Toolbar opens and exposes icons representing various tools (Figure 1.9). One of the available tools is the Spotlight. The Spotlight may not appear in the default Floating Tools Toolbar. If it does not, you need to add it by clicking on the Customize icon, which looks a bit like a gear.

Touch or click and drag the Spotlight icon to the Floating Tools Toolbar. You can place it anywhere you like on the toolbar. A blue line appears on the Floating Tools Toolbar to identify where the Spotlight icon will be placed. On the Spotlight icon itself you will see + and a shaded rectangle representing the object right before it is added to the Floating Tools Toolbar. Select Done in the customization menu to close the menu.

Figure 1.9. Customizing the Floating Tools Toolbar

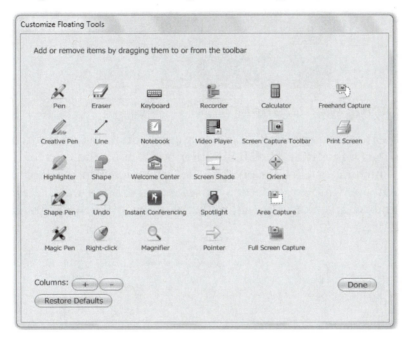

To access the Spotlight with the website you would like to examine open, touch or click on the Spotlight icon and it will appear on your screen (Figure 1.10, page 12). The Spotlight can be shrunk or enlarged by touching the blue edge of it and while maintaining pressure, either pulling away from the center to enlarge or pushing towards the center to shrink. You can move the Spotlight by touching the Spotlight on the screen (not the one in the toolbar). By maintaining pressure and moving the Spotlight on the board, it will move the spotlight focus area.

There are additional adjustments you can make by finding the triangle down arrow on the Spotlight that appears on your screen. Touching the down arrow will reveal the options to adjust the transparency and shape of the Spotlight. Touching the word Transparency will reveal options to choose from some to no transparency and selecting the word Shape will give you the option to use a rectangle, ellipse, or star. The final option is Exit. Choosing Exit closes the Spotlight. Another way to exit the Spotlight is to click on the escape (Esc) key if you are at your computer.

Figure 1.10. The Spotlight Tool

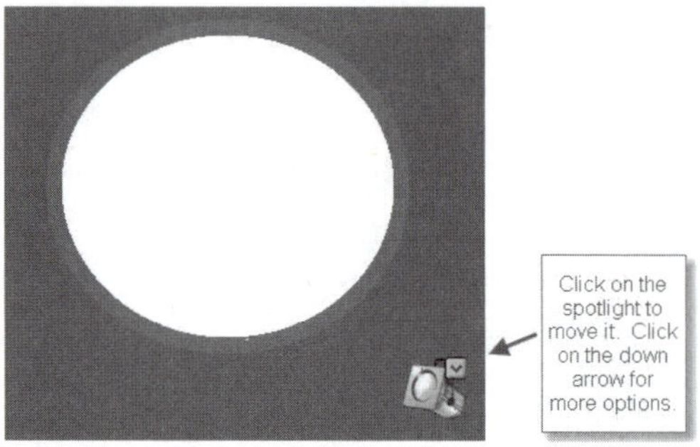

Click on the spotlight to move it. Click on the down arrow for more options.

Using the Highlighter Tool

Another tool you can use to focus students' attention on a particular page feature is the Highlighter. The Highlighter is also found in the Floating Tools Toolbar. Touching or clicking on the Hide/Reveal icon on the Floating Tools Toolbar will open and expose icons representing various tools. The icon with the pen and what looks to be yellow highlighter ink is the Highlighter tool (Figure 1.11).

Figure 1.11. Customizing the Highlighter Tool

The Highlighter tool can be customized. Make sure to Save Tool Properties if you want the change to apply to the toolbar.

Properties

Fill Effects

Line Style

Color

More...

Thickness

Save Tool Properties

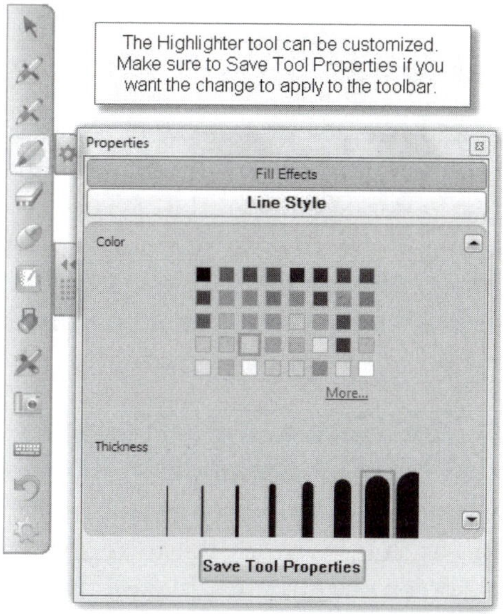

Touching the Highlighter tool with your finger or clicking with a mouse activates it. You will see what looks like a screen outline or secondary layer appear around the edge of the screen. This is called the Digital Ink Layer and it will allow you to write or highlight anything on the website and later save your notes (Figure 1.12).

Figure 1.12. Digital Ink Layer

Digital Ink Layer Border

Clear writing

Capture writing

Close Digital Ink Layer

Once the Digital Ink Layer is activated, the next thing that you touch on the screen will be highlighted. You will continue to highlight anything you touch on the screen until you touch the Select icon in the Floating Tools Toolbar. If you would like to, you can also write any notes, draw lines, etc., on the web page. To do so, select a pen from the Floating Tools Toolbar by touching the color you would like to use. The next place you touch on the board, you will be able to write or draw. Make any annotations on the page that you would like as you examine the age with your students. When you are finished, touch the Select icon to deactivate the pen.

Saving Internet Resources

At this point, you will need to decide whether or not you would like to save your notes. Three icons appear in the upper right-hand corner of the screen of the Digital Ink Layer (see Figure 1.12). The red X icon to the far right closes the Digital Ink Layer, deleting all of your notes with it. If you do not want to save your notes or are done using the site, that is the icon to press. The icon to the far left that looks like paper with a sun on it will clear any of the digital writing that you had on the page and give you a fresh digital ink layer.

If you would like to save your notes, click on the middle Screen Capture icon. Doing so will take a screen shot of all of your notes and transfer it to your last opened Notebook file. You may also want to copy the URL of the website and save it in case you would like to return to the site later and to cite the source of your screen shot in your file. Before minimizing the website page, copy the URL and then return to the Notebook file. You will see the screen shot of the website you took your notes on in one of the pages of your Notebook file.

Citing Web Resources and Linking

To cite the Internet source of the screen shot you inserted into the Notebook file, you have two options.

First, you can paste the website address onto the Notebook page. To copy the address, drag your finger over the top of it to select the whole address. With the On-Screen Keyboard, you can then touch the Ctrl button and then the letter C. This will copy the address. Alternatively, touch the board maintaining pressure for a few seconds. Doing so will act as a right-click would at your computer. You can also click on the mouse button in the pen tray or in your Floating Tools toolbar and the next touch on the screen will be a right-click. You will see a drop-down menu and you will be able to choose Copy from it. To paste the address onto your workspace in Notebook, open the page you would like to put it on. You can now use the On-Screen Keyboard to paste the website address on the page by touching the Ctrl button and then the letter V. You can also access the paste option through a right-click action on your board. When you complete the process you will see the website address on your screen. Touching the object with some pressure allows you to move it. You can also use the gray handle in the lower right-hand corner when the object is active to shrink or increase the size of it. If you are at your computer and would like to adjust the font, you can double-click on the text and an active text box will appear. First highlight the text in the text box with your mouse, then select the font you would like to use. Click on the Select icon in the main toolbar and your text box will return to being an object that you can move around on the page. A second option allows you to link the website address to the object and hide the actual website address from view. To do so, make sure you have copied the address from the web page and have returned to the Notebook file where your screen shot is saved. Touch the screen shot object with pressure until you see the dashed blue lines around the edge of the object and the triangle icon for the drop-down menu appear. Touch the triangle icon and from the drop-down menu and select Link. A new menu appears. The first option in the menu is for a web address. Click on the space below where it says Address and paste the web address there. If you are at your computer, you can accomplish the same task by pasting the URL into the Address box using your Ctrl commands or making use of the right-click menu.

You will notice that the link to Web Page option in the lower part of the menu is automatically selected, as well as the launch by clicking the corner icon. Clicking on the OK button will return you to the Notebook page, where you will see a globe in the lower left-hand corner of the screen shot object. In most cases, it seems to be better if you leave the launch defaulted to show the corner icon, that way you will know that the object is linked to an Internet site. If you do not, you will not see a corner icon and it will not be evident that the object is linked until you click on it. You can test the link by touching the corner icon. If everything was done correctly, you will be automatically taken to the website. Although it may take a little extra time, going through the citation process with students reinforces good practice for crediting information sources and may save you time later.

Adjusting Screen Shot Size

If the screen shot of the website is not centered the way you would like on the Notebook page, touch the object (the screen shot) and you will see a blue dashed line around the edge of the object. This means you can move it. Move the object where you would like on the page. If it is too big, look for the gray handle (in the form of a circle) in the lower right-hand corner of the object. By touching and maintaining pressure on the handle, you can shrink the size of it by moving your finger toward the center of the object. Pulling your finger toward the bottom right of the screen enlarges the object.

Using the Screen Capture Tool

Another tool found in the Floating Tools Toolbar is the Screen Capture tool (Figure 1.13, page 16). This tool allows you to capture a portion or all of a web page that is viewable in the frame of your computer monitor or on the interactive whiteboard. If it is not in the default settings for your toolbar, you will need to touch or click on the Customize icon in the Floating Tools Toolbar, select the Screen Capture icon which looks like a camera, and add it to your Floating Tools Toolbar. More specific instructions on customizing the Floating Tools Toolbar are found in the earlier section discussing the Spotlight. With the web page from which you would like to capture something open, touch the Screen Capture icon in the Floating Tools Toolbar. A small window will pop up that includes four capture options. The one furthest to the left will allow you to capture a portion of a page.

The capture icon that is second from the left will allow you to capture a specific window of a screen. The icon with a blue background that is second from the right will capture the full screen and the fourth capture tool that is closest to the right allows a freehand capture where you can control the shape of what you are capturing. Although the Digital Ink Layer will allow you to capture the full screen along with your notes, the four Screen Capture tool options found in the Floating Tools Toolbar allow more flexibility if you are only interested in capturing a selection of text, a portion of the page, part

Figure 1.13. Capture Tools

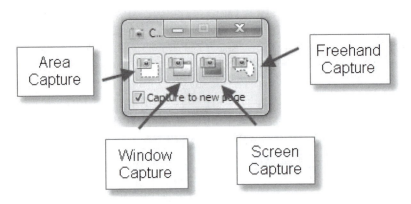

of an image, or an image that may only be added to Notebook with a Screen Capture tool. The Screen Capture tool will work with any screen that you have on your computer from word processing documents to the Notebook software itself.

Version 10.6 Additional Features

An additional feature of version 10.6 allows you to make the Notebook software transparent, but still have access to the content of the page, as well as many of the tools from the main toolbar. To make the Notebook transparent, click on the icon in the main toolbar that has a screen and a gray-and-white checkerboard pattern in it (Figure 1.14). You will see the content from the Notebook page on your screen superimposed over anything else on your screen, but will not see the Notebook software itself. Clicking on the Transparent Background icon pops up a toolbar. The Transparent Mode Toolbar (Figure 1.15) provides the features shown in Figures 1.12 (page 13) and 1.13. The Transparent Mode icon is not available if you are working on a Macintosh.

Figure 1.14. Transparent Background Tool

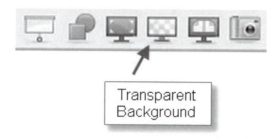

Figure 1.15. Transparent Background Floating Toolbar

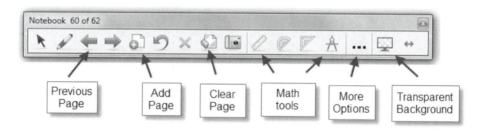

This toolbar gives you access to the math and other visible tools for interacting with the website. The More Options icon, represented by the ... in the toolbar, allows you to access many other tools from the standard toolbar of Notebook, including the various pen and highlighter tools and tools to add lines, shapes, and a screen shade, as well as the options to undo and redo performed actions. Any writing you do will appear on the page of the Notebook file when you leave the Transparent Background mode. If you are working with an Internet page that you would like to save, you will need to use the Capture tool to add the content to Notebook. Click on the red X in the toolbar or the Transparent Background icon to exit the Transparent Background mode.

Conclusion

Sometimes the simplest uses of a tool can be the most powerful. This first chapter started with combining a good question to get students thinking and using basic tools of the interactive whiteboard like pens, highlighters and a spotlight to support the discussion process. Adding in the interactivity the board provides for examining Internet resources and the ability to easily capture those resources for later use are other valuable ways to help students to explore their questions.

2

Integrate Multiple Forms of Media

Idea 3: Use Images

Purposes for Using Images

Images are powerful. There is a wealth of image resources available at your fingertips in your own photo collections and online, as well as in the clip art collections you have in the Notebook Gallery, online, and in other sources you may have. Images can be used for many purposes:

- ♦ To create an emotional connection to the subject.
- ♦ To show visual representation of people and their cultures:
  - • Compare and contrast elements of different cultures.
- ♦ To generate interest when introducing a new idea, concept or lesson:
  - • Cover part of the image to build curiosity about what is missing.
- ♦ As a discussion generator:
  - • Pose a question or questions about a thought-provoking image.
  - • Ask students to come up with their own questions about the image or why you chose it to illustrate what you are presenting.
- ♦ As a writing prompt.
- ♦ To help explain a concept that is better represented pictorially.
- ♦ To help teach language with picture-text associations.
- ♦ To add humor to a lesson.
- ♦ To get students to think:

- Pair two seemingly unrelated images together and ask students to find a connection between them.

Finding Images

It is generally more efficient to search for images on your computer, than on the interactive whiteboard. You can very quickly do one of the aforementioned things with an image and it takes only as long as needed to find the image. The first thing to determine is your purpose in using the image. There are many resources for finding images, but looking in locations listed below should give you some ideas on where to start. As you search, make sure the images you are selecting are of good quality and not distorted. Also make sure to cite the image source as you add images to your lesson.

Photos

- ◆ Your own digital photo collections. You may have traveled somewhere or seen something that is relevant to your lesson. Using your own photos may be a way to personalize your lesson as well.
- ◆ Online photo collections
  - *Google Images:* http://images.google.com/

    Limit your search by the content and whether you are looking for photos or clip art
  - *Flickr:* http://www.flickr.com/
  - *Picasa:* http://picasa.google.com/
  - *Photobucket:* http://photobucket.com/
  - *Library of Congress American Memory Collection:* http://memory.loc.gov/ammem/index.html

    Particularly useful for primary source images and documents on U.S. history

Clip Art

- ◆ Your own clip art collections
- ◆ The Gallery of the Notebook software
- ◆ Word processing clip art collections
- ◆ Online clip art sources
  - *Google Images:* http://images.google.com/

- *Discovery Education Clip Art:* http://school.discoveryeducation.com/clip art/

- *Florida Educational Technology Clearinghouse:* http://etc.usf.edu/clip art/

Adding Images to Notebook Files

Once you have found an image that you would like to use, there are three ways to put it into the Notebook file.

1. Right-click on the image and choose Copy Image. Open the page in Notebook onto which you would like to place the image. Use the shortcut Ctrl + V to paste or right-click on the Notebook workspace and choose Paste.

2. With some pictures you will be able to click on them and drag them into the Notebook workspace. To do this effectively, you need to tile the windows of the website you are taking the image from and the Notebook file. Tile the windows by minimizing the size of each window so you can view them side by side. Click on the image and drag it into the workspace in Notebook.

3. A third way to bring a picture into Notebook is by inserting it. This works well when you have an image, be it clip art or photo, saved in your files. In Notebook, select the Insert menu to get the drop-down menu. Chose Picture File as your option. You will then be prompted to browse through your files to find the image you would like to use. Select the image you would like and click Open. Your image will then insert itself into the Notebook workspace.

Resizing the Image

If the image you insert is larger than what you would like it to be, click on the image and you will see the dashed blue lines around the edge and the gray handle in the lower right-hand corner of the image. Click on the handle and drag it toward the center of the object if it is too big. Drag it toward the lower right-hand corner of the page if it is too small. Holding down the Shift key while you adjust the object size ensures that the image keeps its original dimensions and avoids distortions.

Editing the Image

When you use clip art from sources other than the Gallery, you may find that it has a white area around the image itself. Once you start changing the page background colors, you may find that it isn't visually appealing to have the white background surrounding the image. You can remove the white background by right-clicking on the clip art and choosing Set Picture Transparency from the drop-down menu. When you select this function, the clip art pops up in a new window and you are directed to click on the areas that you want to make transparent. Click on all of the white areas that you want to remove. When you are satisfied with the changes, select OK. When you add a colored page background, you will no longer see the white area. If you find that you missed a white area of the clip art, repeat the process.

Adding Images to the Gallery

Before you move on, you should decide if the image you inserted into the Notebook file is one that you would like to use again in the future. If so, you will want to click on the Gallery tab (Figure 2.1).

Figure 2.1. The Gallery Tab

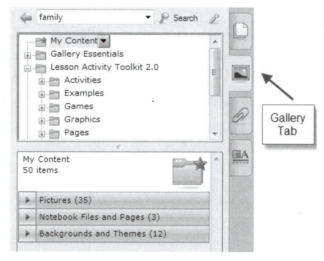

Once the Gallery tab is open, click on the folder labeled My Content. In the larger space below you will see a listing of what is in the My Content folder. Click on the triangle arrow that is facing to the right in the area labeled My Pictures to expose the contents of the folder. Upon doing so, the triangle arrow turns blue and faces toward the lower right-hand corner. You will also see any images that are in the folder. With the folder open, click on the image you would like to add to your content in the Gallery. Once you click on it, you can drag it into the open area under the Pictures bar. It is a good idea to rename the picture to something that will be easily identifiable to you the next time you search for it. To do so, click once on the text that is immediately below the picture. The text box will activate and you can type in the label you would like the picture to have.

Linking Images to their Sources

It is always a good idea to cite the source of an image. You always want to give credit to the source of the image and you never know when you might need to find the website the image came from in the future. You have a couple of options for linking the object to its source (Figure 2.2). You can do it immediately before you add the object to the Gallery or you can add the link and then add it to the Gallery. If you add the link first, no matter what file you reuse the image in, it will always have the link attached to it. If you add the image to the Gallery first and then add the link to the image in the Notebook workspace, the link will only be active in that specific file.

Remember that to add a link to an image you need to click on the image once. Click on the down arrow. A second option is to right-click on the image directly and the drop-down menu will appear immediately. From the drop-down menu, select Link (Figure 2.2). A new window will pop up and you will need to copy and paste the web site address into the Address box (Figure 2.3, page 26). You will then need to decide whether you want the whole object to link to its source when clicking on the corner icon or when the object itself is clicked. Be aware that if you link the object itself to its source, any time you touch anywhere on that object, you will be redirected to the web site. You can also link any text to its source in the same way.

Figure 2.2. Adding a Link to an Object

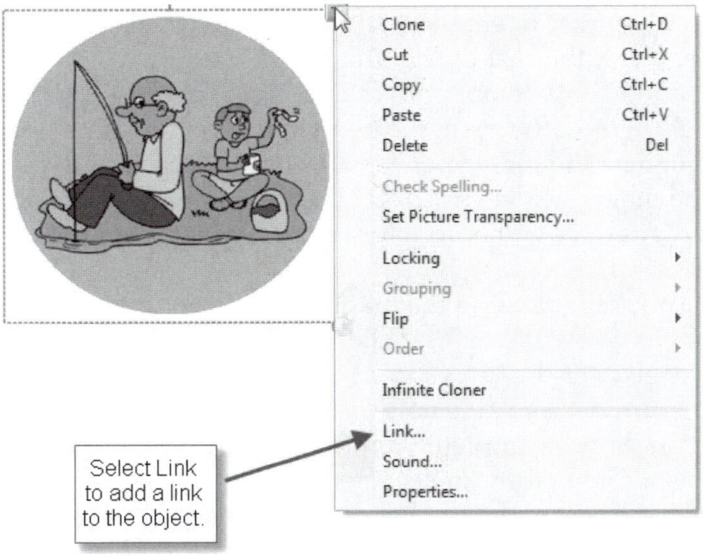

Clone	Ctrl+D
Cut	Ctrl+X
Copy	Ctrl+C
Paste	Ctrl+V
Delete	Del
Check Spelling...	
Set Picture Transparency...	
Locking	▶
Grouping	▶
Flip	▶
Order	▶
Infinite Cloner	
Link...	
Sound...	
Properties...	

Select Link to add a link to the object.

Figure 2.3. Insert Link

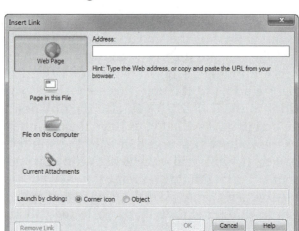

Using Images in a Lesson

Once you have collected some images, you will need to decide how to arrange them on the page. If the image is the focus of the page for your lesson activity, you may want to consider only putting one image on each page, as that will get students to focus solely on that one image. If you want students to examine the image in more detail, you can use the Spotlight tool discussed in Chapter 1 to get them to focus on particular areas of the image while blocking out the rest of the image. You can access the Spotlight tool from the Floating Tools Toolbar or you can create one with the magic pen. To create the Spotlight with the magic pen, first select it from the main toolbar. You will recognize the magic pen because it has stars around the edge of a pen tool. The magic pen is "magical" because when you write on the page with it, the digital ink will automatically disappear from the page within a few seconds.

To create a spotlight using the magic pen, draw a circle. When you complete the circle, you will see that the spotlight forms. Move the spotlight around the page over the image to have students focus in what you would like them to examine. As a side note, if you do use the magic pen for writing, make sure you do not complete your zeros or the letter O perfectly or they will create a spotlight. You can also create a magnifying tool with the magic pen by drawing a rectangle on the part of the image that you would like to magnify. When you complete the drawing of the rectangle, that portion of the image appears magnified. Click anywhere on the blue edge of the magnifier to move it around the page. Click on the magnifier and drag your mouse to the right to further magnify the image. To decrease the magnification, click and drag your mouse to the left.

Generally, the maximum number of images to use on a page is four. There are, of course, times when more images are appropriate, but the more you have to fit on the page the smaller they have to be. When in doubt, you may just want to make another page and add the images there.

Adding Sound Files to Images

Adding Existing Sounds

Many websites offer sound clip downloads. Some are free and others may charge a per download fee or offer package or yearly prices. Doing an Internet search for the best free sound effects may also help. You may also want to search Richard Byrne's site: http://www.freetech4teachers.com/ for *55 Places for Free Sound Effects* for an annotated list of other sound resources. Here are a few sites to get you started:

♦ *Find Sounds:* http://www.findsounds.com/

♦ *SoundBible:* http://soundbible.com/

♦ *FlashKit:* http://flashkit.com/soundfx/

When looking for sounds, you need to look for MP3 files if you want to be able to embed the sound into the object or image. Download the MP3 files you would like to use and save them in a folder that you can easily find.

To add sound to any object in Notebook, including images and text, right-click and choose Sound from the drop-down menu (Figure 2.4).

Figure 2.4. Adding Sound to an Object

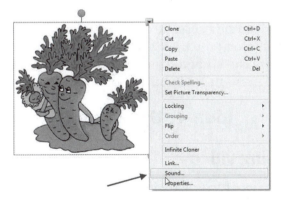

A new window will pop up in which you will be asked to Browse for the sound (Figure 2.5, page 28). Once you find the sound, choose it and select Open. Clicking on the Play button allows you to preview the sound. You now need to decide if you want to have the sound play when you click the object or the corner icon. If you choose the corner icon option, a small speaker icon will display on the bottom left side of the image. Choose OK to apply the sound. Should you decide that you would like to change the sound or the settings later on, you can once again choose Sound in the drop-down menu and remove the sound completely, change the sound, or adjust the directions for playing the sound.

Figure 2.5. Insert Sound

Creating Your Own Sound Files

There are many sound recording programs available for you to record your voice or other sounds. The Garage Band application available on the Macintosh has features that allow you to record your voice and then alter it. It also allows you to create your own music. If you are looking for a free resource that works on both the Mac and the PC, Audacity (http://audacity. sourceforge.net/) offers the ability to record your voice, edit the tracks, and silence out any background noise. To convert the Audacity files to MP3 files, you need to also download the LAME encoder. Once you record the file and save it as an MP3, you can embed it into objects in the Notebook file by using the directions in the previous section.

Idea 4: Use Videos

Purposes for Using Videos

There many sources for video clips available online and through subscription services. Generally speaking, showing shorter video clips with frequent pauses for discussion is more effective than showing a long video. Video clips offer flexibility in that you can choose a key point that you want students to understand and then discuss the clip. Their smaller sizes make it convenient to save them in the Notebook file with the rest of your lesson and can improve your lesson flow and organization. Depending on the students' level and your lesson purpose, you can adjust the number of clips you use during any given class period.

The accessibility of video clips also opens up opportunities to use video as part of a lesson where you may not previously have considered doing so. Talking about a topic and including a visual representation and explanation can increase student engagement in the lesson, as well as deepen their understanding of and connections to the topic.

Types of Videos

Every day the number of video clips available online dramatically increases because of the culture of sharing on the Internet. Some ideas for types of videos you might look for are instructional videos to:

- ◆ Build background knowledge on a topic
  - Content knowledge
  - Vocabulary
- ◆ Explain a concept or demonstrate a process
  - Grammatical
  - Scientific
  - Mathematical
  - Writing
  - Engineering
  - Mechanical
- ◆ Develop cultural understanding
  - Documentaries
  - Food preparation and meals
  - Weather reports
  - Representations of daily life, holidays, and celebrations
  - Music videos and clips from shows and concerts
- ◆ Promote discussion
- ◆ Promote further student inquiry about the topic
- ◆ Teach through song and play

◆ Show students examples to model work created by other students

Finding Videos

The first time you start searching for videos can be a bit overwhelming. You may not be sure where to look or how to convert the videos to a useable format. Before you begin your video search, have a clear idea of what type of content you are looking for, as there will be many opportunities to detour, some educationally valuable and others more entertaining. Because YouTube is so well known, that is the first stop for many video searchers. Although there is valuable content there, your school may have limited access to that site so you cannot depend on just going to the site and streaming the video. Your school may also not want you to stream video, depending upon your school's bandwith. Although there are sites that will convert files from YouTube, they do violate the terms of use of the site. The good thing is that there are many alternatives to YouTube that are educationally appropriate.

Below are a few video sites to get you started, but you may also want to take a look at the research on alternatives to YouTube done by Richard Byrne at http://www.freetech4teachers.com/ entitled *30+ Alternatives to YouTube*. Some videos you find you will be able to directly download, others will need to be converted, and the terms of use of others require that you stream the content from the website they are stored on. News networks like CNN and the BBC are also great places to look for current events and other content in video clip form. Some ideas on sites to check out for videos are:

◆ *How Stuff Works:* http://www.howstuffworks.com/

Extensive collection of video clips that explain how things work.

◆ *Big Think:* http://bigthink.com/

Includes a collection of interviews with experts from around the world on multiple topics including, Arts and Culture, Business and Economics, Environment, History, Identity, Truth and Justice.

◆ *Snag Films:* http://www.snagfilms.com/

Offers documentaries on multiple topics including the Arts, History, Politics, Culture, Science and Nature, War, Women's Issues.

◆ *Library of Congress Webcasts:* http://www.loc.gov/today/cyberlc/youtube.html

Offers webcasts from the Library of Congress on Biography, History, Religion, Science, Technology, and more.

- *Dot Sub:* http://dotsub.com/

  Offers videos in multiple languages that have been subtitled for other languages.

- *Common Craft:* http://www.commoncraft.com/

  Simple explanations of topics like blogs, wikis, and podcasting.

- *Teacher's TV:* http://www.teachers.tv/

  Offers methods and instructional videos to teachers in the United Kingdom.

If it does not violate the terms of service of the website, you can use www.zamzar.com to convert online videos to play in QuickTime and other players. There are multiple conversion formats from which to choose. Converting the file to a file with the extension .mov or .mp4 will play in most players.

Adding Videos to Notebook Files

You may find it handy to attach video files directly to your lesson so everything is stored in one place and easy to find. One way to add a video file in an .mp4 or .mov format to a Notebook lesson, is to start by opening the Attachments tab of the Notebook file. Once the Attachments tab is open, select Insert. Three options will appear: Insert Copy of File, Insert Hyperlink, Insert Shortcut to File (Figure 2.6). In most instances you will want to choose Insert Copy of File.

Figure 2.6. Insert Attachment

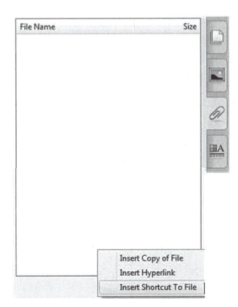

This is the most flexible option for opening the file because if you insert a shortcut to the file you will only be able to access that file when you are on the same computer the file is located. If you always plan to save and work from the same computer, it may not be a problem for you and it can save on file size. If you decide that you would like to link the file to an object later on, as is described below, you can still do so. When it comes time to use the video clip, you can go to the Attachments file. Double-clicking on the video opens it in the media player that is installed on your computer. (Talk to your technology support specialists at your school if you are not sure what media player your school uses.)

Another way to embed a video file in the Notebook lesson is by attaching it to an object. The object can be text, a shape, or an image. The process is very similar to that of adding a link to an object as shown earlier in Figures 2.2 (page 25) and 2.3 (page 26). Once you have the object on the page you would like to attach the video to, right-click on the object and select Link. When asked to choose from the options at the left, choose File on this Computer, unless you have a copy in the Attachments. If you choose File on this Computer, a new menu will pop up and asking you to browse for the file to which you would like to link. Select the file you would like and click Open. You can also choose to insert the file as a copy or a shortcut and decide whether you would like touching the object or the corner icon to cause the file to open. When you are done, click OK. You will know the file has attached when you see a paperclip icon in the lower left-hand corner of the object.

Saving the File to the Gallery

It is possible to save the video file to the Gallery if you have attached it to an object (shape, image, or text). To add it to the Gallery, make sure that you have the My Content folder open, with the blue arrow pointing to the lower right-hand corner. Drag the object to the Gallery. You will want to rename the file by clicking once on the text below it once it is in the Gallery. This will enable you to search for the video.

Documenting Video Sources

The Insert Hyperlink option found in the Attachments area allows you to save the address of a website. You may find it useful to use this feature to document the source of any videos you are using. To add a hyperlink, click on the Attachments tab and then select Insert. From your options choose Insert Hyperlink. A new window will pop up asking for the hyperlink. Copy and paste the web address that is the source of your video. In the box entitled Display Name, type the title of the video. Another option is to have a page in your Notebook file that identifies the video and its source in a bibliography.

A Few Benefits of Showing Videos on the Interactive Whiteboard

Because you are showing digital videos, you can easily pause and rewind to review an important point. You can also pause the video and write on the still image with the interactive whiteboard pen to identify any important vocabulary, process, or element that is depicted. You can also pause the video at a particular point and use the still image to ask questions about it and/or use it as a starting point for a discussion. Being able to view the videos on the large screen of the interactive whiteboard also adds to the experience. When the video is paused, you can also use the Screen Capture tool to capture an image or multiple images from the video. You can use the images to prompt a discussion before or after viewing, ask students to describe what is going on in the image, use a selection of the images for an ordering activity and more, depending upon your purpose.

Conclusion

There is a wealth of existing resource material just waiting to be found on the Internet. Stepping away from the limitations of a television and a DVD player and having an interactive whiteboard opens up many new options. Rather than watching a video in its entirety, you can quickly show a series of short video clips on a topic, easily stopping for discussion. The interactive whiteboard even allows you to write on the video itself to draw students' attention to a particular feature and spark a discussion. Although this chapter focuses primarily on resources for finding images and videos and how to add them into a Notebook presentation, it is important to remember that other types of media resources are available to you and your students. Using a variety of media will help students stay engaged. If you don't already use the following you may also want to consider looking for:

♦ Podcasts

   ITunes U has many educational podcasts, in addition to the others you can find from other online sources.

♦ Screencasts

   There are many screencasting tools that allow the user to both record their voice and capture a video of the individual demonstrating a process on a computer screen.

♦ Voice Threads

   Creators of Voice Threads can use images or video along with textual or audio commentary to present material. Other users with access to the Voice Thread can also leave comments.

◆ Other Presentations and Games Templates

There are many shared presentations, like PowerPoints, already online. Just because you now have the software that accompanies your interactive whiteboard does not mean you have to stop using prior resources or transfer them into the software your interactive whiteboard uses. Show the presentation or play the game on the interactive whiteboard in its original form. Remember that variety is a good thing.

3

Interact with Online Resources

Idea 5: Use Online Resources

Learning is both more fun and more interesting when students can interact with the material they are learning. Quality interactive online resources that appeal to your students are a way to engage them while using the interactive whiteboard in whole-class and small-group learning experiences. Every day more interactive online resources are added to the Internet. The rate at which this collection of resources grows is both astounding and, at times, overwhelming. This chapter samples the types of resources that are available to facilitate interactive instruction in your classroom using these web-based resources. It is up to you to look at the resources for your particular discipline and evaluate their usefulness for your students. Some may work well for whole-group instruction, whereas others may meet the needs of a smaller group of your students. Although many of the resources in this chapter may continue to develop and stay current, some may not. The intention of the included links is to give you a place to start and give you a sense of the kinds of resources that are available. To keep up with regularly updated resources online you may want to follow Richard Byrne on his site: http://www.freetech4teachers.com/. You may also want to check out José Picardo's updates to his Resources section of his website: http://www.boxoftricks.net/. There are, of course, many other awesome online resources, but the Byrne and Picardo sites provide a starting point. The resources provided in this book are as follows:

- ◆ Presentational Resources
  - Presentation Sharing Sites
  - Interactive Whiteboard Lesson Sharing Sites
- ◆ Research and Discovery Resources
  - Virtual Explorations
  - Primary Source Documents and Images
  - Government-Sponsored Resources

- ◆ Skills Practice Resources
  - • Interactive Web Resources
  - • Online Books and Stories
  - • Websites to Create your own Content
- ◆ Global Connection Resources
  - • Skype
  - • Google Earth
  - • Epals

Presentational Resources

Presentation Sharing Sites

To find existing resources for presenting new topics to students, you can certainly use your favorite search engine to perform a specific search for the materials you need. You can also use presentation sharing sites. Remember that although you can use the sites to find, create, and share instructional resources, students can also use them to share their own work with an authentic audience. Because these sharing sites are accessed and contributed to globally, you can use them to find resources created by people with different cultural perspectives and in different languages. Sharing your own presentations is a way to contribute your work to the global community and another way to support student learning outside of class, as it allows students another opportunity to review the material. An additional benefit of the presentation sharing sites is that you can store your work online and access it from anywhere with Internet access. A few places for presentation sharing are listed below.

- ◆ http://www.pppst.com/

  Pete's PowerPoint Station has PowerPoint presentations for many subject areas and topics. It also includes links to interactive games.

- ◆ www.slideshare.net

  This sharing site is one of the best known and as a result has a large selection of presentation resources.

- ◆ www.prezi.com

  This sharing tool organizes presentational information a bit differently than your standard linear presentation sharing site. Check into a free educator account.

♦ http://photopeach.com/

Find and create photo slide shows with audio and captions.

New sharing services are regularly added to the Internet. The four listed are just a few to get you started. You will want to evaluate the individual sites and services based on the resources they have for your content area, your purpose in using it, and the features you are looking for. To explore and compare other presentational sharing sites, you may want to check out the posting on www.freetech4teachers.com entitled *12 Ways for Students to Publish Slideshows Online.*

Interactive Whiteboard Lesson-Sharing Sites

As interactive whiteboards become more accessible in classrooms, the collection of shared interactive whiteboard lessons and activities expands. If you are not quite ready to create a lesson of your own or would like to see some ideas on how others have used the tools, you may want to check out the resources on the sites that follow. As you look at any of the lessons you find, evaluate them for quality. You may want to ask yourself the following questions as you look at the lessons and activities:

♦ Do they include opportunities for students to actively interact with the lesson material physically and/or mentally?

♦ Do they include any multimedia elements beyond text such as objects, images, audio, video, Flash-based activities, and/or links to interactive websites, or do they look like something that could just as well be accomplished on a worksheet?

♦ Do they use color, text, and images well, and is the content easy to see for students in the back of your classroom?

♦ Would this lesson work well for whole-group instruction or would it work to meet the needs of a smaller group of my students?

Websites that include SMART Notebook lessons for download are as follows:

♦ http://education.smarttech.com/ste/en-US/Ed+Resource/

From SMART Technologies, this area includes many resources for getting started with lesson creation. Check out the Lesson Activities section to find Notebook lessons created by educators who work for SMART.

♦ http://exchange.smarttech.com/index.html

Hosted by SMART Technologies, the SMART Exchange is a collection of lessons contributed by teachers for different subject areas.

♦ http://iwbrevolution.ning.com/

The Interactive Whiteboard Revolution Ning is an online community of educators learning and sharing ideas about interactive whiteboard use. It includes a space for sharing lessons.

♦ http://smartboardtips.wikispaces.com/

The SMART Tips Wiki includes sample Notebook files for different content areas, game templates, and links to other Notebook files and interactive content.

♦ http://www.interactivewhiteboard.net.au/

This Australian website provides Notebook lessons for a variety of content areas, as well as a selection of other related resources.

You can also find lesson resources by doing a search using your preferred search engine. When doing the searches, use the keywords of the content you are looking for or be more general by using the subject area itself. Along with your subject-specific search term you will also want to try the keywords "SMART Board," "interactive whiteboard," and "Notebook lessons" in your searches. If you are using a different brand of interactive whiteboard, you will want to use the general term "interactive whiteboard" and the brand -pecific name for the product as part of your searches.

Research and Discovery Resources

Virtual Explorations

It used to be that you needed to be in physical attendance to experience and enjoy the richness of museums, art galleries, and unknown places. Now you can use the big screen of the interactive whiteboard as a portal to transport your students to places they might not otherwise have the opportunity to explore. The interactive whiteboard can be the tool that allows students to view and examine those places and the features of them to help them better understand their world. This section highlights various resources you can use to engage in virtual explorations.

♦ http://www.si.edu/

The Smithsonian offers its own rich encyclopedia with written, visual, and audio resources. Visit online collections at the museums and access lesson plans, teaching resources, and idea lab activities for students. View videos on the Smithsonian Channel, access research resources through their collections files of images, sound, and videos, and much more!

♦ http://www.nga.gov/

National Gallery of Art in Washington, DC offers online tours, podcasts, videos, images, and information about the art from their collections.

♦ http://www.fi.edu/learn/hotlists/art.php

This site provides links to many art galleries and other art resources.

The images, documents, videos, podcasts, and other information available through the websites above can be used to introduce a new unit and spark some questions about the topic, as part of the main lesson content of the unit, or as resources for students to do their own exploration and research of a topic of personal interest to them. The resources can serve as writing prompts and visuals for formative assessments along the way, as well as parts of summative assessments after students have concluded the unit.

Primary Source Documents and Images

Of the many quality research and discovery resources on the Internet with which students can interact, primary source documents are very valuable ones. The increasing availability of primary source documents and images allows both teachers and students to examine resources that previously were much less accessible. As a result of the hard work of many dedicated individuals, resources that were previously only available to view in person at museums and other repositories are now available to the public through the click of a mouse. Now students can see scanned versions of those same documents first-hand and start to build the skills to look at materials the way historians do. What makes the process even better is that most of the documents and images can be downloaded and saved. Adding them to a Notebook file to use for future lessons can be as easy as copying and pasting the resource to a Notebook page or attaching a document to the Attachments tab and citing the source of the material. The Notebook file allows easy storage and presentation of the resources. Here are some sources in the United States where you can find primary source documents and images:

♦ http://www.loc.gov/index.html

Explore the Digital Collections area of the Library of Congress to find print, pictorial, and audiovisual collections.

♦ http://www.ourdocuments.gov

This site provides 100 primary source documents, including the Declaration of Independence and the Bill of Rights.

♦ http://www.memorialhall.mass.edu/home.html

Memorial Hall Museum and Library, one of the United States' oldest museums, offers an impressive collection of primary source documents online, interactive hands-on activities, online exhibitions, and educator resources.

♦ http://www.digitalhistory.uh.edu/

This comprehensive site on American history includes many resources, such as primary source documents created by the Department of History and College of Education at the University of Houston.

Government-Sponsored Resources

The United States government also supports a variety of sites that provide valuable learning resources. Depending upon the level of the students you teach and the lesson purpose, you may want to add one of the site resources to a page of your interactive whiteboard lesson, link to it to do an initial exploration of the site as a class, or allow students to direct their own exploration of the site. Check out the annotations of the sites to find out what each has to offer.

♦ http://www.kids.gov/

This is the official site of the United States Government for kids. It has links to more than 2,000 websites, including government agencies, schools and educational agencies. It is divided into K–5, 6–8, and Educator resources.

♦ http://free.ed.gov/

This site offers more than 1,500 free, federally supported learning resources, including animations, primary source documents, photos, and videos. Contributors include NASA, the National Science Foundation, National Institutes of Health, the National Endowment of the Humanities, the National Archives, the Library of Congress, and more.

- https://www.cia.gov/library/publications/the-world-fact-book/

  The CIA World Factbook provides factual country profile information, as well as a map, flag, and some visual images for each country.

- http://www.usa.gov/Citizen/Topics/Education_Training/Teacher_Resources.shtml

  Access educationally valuable resources from the U.S. government, including information about national parks, the census, the federal court system, the Constitution, energy and environmental education resources.

- http://www.thegateway.org/

  The Gateway provides access to a large collection of Internet-based lesson plans and resources from federal, state, university, nonprofit, and commercial Internet sites.

Interactive Skills Practice Resources

Providing opportunities for students to actively engage in their learning is one of the key uses of the interactive whiteboard. Chapter 5 discusses some of the interactive tools that are included in the Notebook software, but you can also take advantage of the many quality interactive resources that already exist on the Internet. As you explore the sites that follow, think about whether or not the resources would lend themselves well to whole-group instruction, might work well for a small-group learning station activity, or might just work well for one particular student who is struggling with a concept. You might find it helpful to use the screen capture tool in Notebook to capture an image from the activity itself that will serve as a visual reminder to you as to what the activity entails. From there you can link the website to the image that represents it in your Notebook file for easy accessibility.

Interactive Websites

- http://www.educational-freeware.com/

  This site reviews free learning games, websites, and software for a variety of content areas.

- http://www.topmarks.co.uk/

  Out of the United Kingdom, this site has a collection of interactive resources to use for most subject areas.

- http://www.hippocampus.org/

  A project of the Monterrey Institute for Technology, this site provides multimedia resources to explain content for most high school and college subjects.

- http://pbskids.org/whiteboard/

  PBS Kids has a collection of games for elementary-level language arts, math, social science, and the arts.

- http://www.internet4classrooms.com/index.htm

  Includes resources for all content areas. Be sure to check out the Grade Level Help for prekindergarten through 8th grade and Links for PreK-12 to search for interactive resources.

- http://www.2learn.ca/

  Four sites that provide interactive resources are linked to this site. Each focuses on a different age level and subject matter.

- http://www.learnalberta.ca/Search.aspx?lang=en

  From Alberta, Canada, this site has interactive content for many subject areas.

- http://www.thinkfinity.org/home.aspx

  Thinkfinity offers lesson plans, interactive activities, and other resources for K-12 classrooms. Thinkfinity has many partners whose sites it also searches, including Read Write Think (http://www.readwritethink.org/), which offers valuable literacy resources.

- http://www.e-learningforkids.org/

  This site has K-6 resources in a variety of subject areas.

- http://www.crickweb.co.uk/

  From the United Kingdom, this site has a variety of interactive content for different ages and subjects.

- http://www.tes.iboard.co.uk/

  From the United Kingdom, this site offers interactive activities to practice content for a variety of subjects.

- http://teacher.scholastic.com/whiteboards/languagearts.htm

  Scholastic has interactive resources for language arts, science, math, and social studies.

- http://www.professorgarfield.org/pgf_home.html

  This site offers both interactive and printable resources for elementary grades in all content areas, with an emphasis on language arts.

- http://www.bgfl.org/bgfl/15.cfm

  This site has interactive resources for most subject areas listed by topic.

- http://www.shodor.org/interactivate/

  This website offers interactive resources for math and science.

- http://nlvm.usu.edu/en/nav/topic_t_1.html

  The National Library of Virtual Manipulatives for Math offers resources to math teachers.

Another great place to check out for resources for the interactive whiteboard is the Teachers Love SMARTBoards website created by James Hollis: http://www.smartboards.typepad.com/. This site also provides links to interactive resources, as well as other tips and tricks for using the interactive whiteboard.

Online Books and Stories

Another resource to explore if you are a language arts teacher are interactive stories. The sites shared below vary in what makes the stories engaging and in the age levels with which the stories will work. As you check them out, you will want to examine whether or not they are appropriate for the ability levels of your readers. Some of the sites will read to the students and others will give the option for the student to do the reading without the audio support. The following are some benefits of being able to read stories online:

- Increases access to books you may not have in your classroom.

- Allows you to find books from other countries and compare and contrast values and perspectives of different cultures through literature.

- Allows you to easily use the pictures from the stories as writing prompts or to spark a discussion.

- Allows you to write on the pages of the book in digital ink. You or your students can identify and discuss new words, highlight lines that rhyme, draw lines to characters mentioned in the story and the illustrations of them, write questions on the page, highlight meaningful passages, and more.

- ◆ Access books in other language for second language learners and for students whose first language is not the primary language in your country.

- ◆ Helps students who may not be able to easily access a library or who have a library with limited resources to find many books to read if they have Internet access at school, a library, and/or home.

- ◆ Provides a wide selection of books to choose from, making it easier to differentiate for different reading levels and making it more likely that students will find something that interests them.

- ◆ Saves money and cuts down the need to have to buy the extra large story books so all students can see well.

- ◆ Helps books come alive as many offer different interactive features.

It does seem that nearly whatever the age, most students do still enjoy having a good book read to them. Online books offer a great way for students to read a class story or have one read to them. Listed below are some sites to check out for reading resources online:

- ◆ http://www.childrenslibrary.org

   One of the goals of the International Children's Digital Library Foundation is to provide books in all languages for children to access so they can read in their native language no matter where they are. Search the "Read Books" section of this site to explore what they have to offer.

- ◆ http://www.ala.org/gwstemplate.cfm?section=greatwebsites &template=/cfapps/gws/default.cfm

   This site from the American Library Association provides many web resources for children. For reading materials in particular, check out the Languages and Literature section.

- ◆ http://read.gov/

   The Library of Congress offers a selection of digitized books, as well as webcasts of authors speaking about their books.

- ◆ http://www.childrensbooksonline.org/index.htm

This site offers a collection of antique books online.

- http://www.rif.org/kids.htm

The Reading is Fundamental site offers a collection of online books for readers 0 to 15 years of age. Reading resources are available in English and Spanish.

- http://www.storyplace.org/

This site offers preschool and elementary level interactive stories with audio in English and Spanish that also include accompanying online and printable activities.

- http://www.starfall.com/

Starfall offers interactive reading resources for building early literacy with audio and visual support.

- http://www.storylineonline.net/

This site, sponsored by the Screen Actors Guild Foundation, provides videos of actors reading popular childhood stories.

- http://plattsburgh.neric.org/oak/smartboard/stories.htm

This site has a collection of interactive stories from a variety of different websites.

- http://www.magickeys.com/books/

This site offers online stories for young children to young adults. Some books have audio available.

Websites to Create Your Own Content

If you would like to create some content of your own using online resources, there are various resources to help you do so. Richard Byrne's website, http://www.freetech4teachers.com, is a good place to consult for ideas. Watch his current postings, but don't forget to check his archived postings as well. If you do not already subscribe to his site in some way, it is likely to be worth your while to do so.

There are many online resources, including templates and websites that will help you put meaningful content into an interactive practice tool that students will enjoy using. The following are free websites that you can use to create games and flashcards for students to review important material from class.

- http://quizlet.com/

  Quizlet offers both teachers and students the ability to create flashcard sets. Teachers can create flashcard sets for their classes that are then shared with the online community. Students can also create accounts and share flashcard sets with their classmates and the web community. What is nice about this site is that the practice activities go beyond just the flashcards and there is a logical practice progression. First students familiarize themselves with the information through flashcards, then they are asked to type in a response to whatever is on the other side of the flashcard. From here students can choose to play a matching game called Scatter, take a computer generated quiz, or play Space Race. For Space Race, students have to type in an answer before the clue gets to the other side of the screen. They also have a Voice Race option allowing students to say the word. This site continues to make improvements to its offerings.

- www.superteachertools.com

  Super Teacher Tools provides Flash-based resources for teachers to use in the classroom. Teachers or students can create Flash Jeopardy, Who Wants to be a Millionaire, Speed Match, Hangman, and Board Games. Teachers can also use the site to generate seating charts, random groups, and select random names.

- http://books.quia.com/shared/

  Although Quia is site that you can use to create your own games and activities for a yearly fee, this area gives you free access to all of the shared activities that have been created by educators for many different subject areas.

- https://www.wrightcity.k12.mo.us/programsdepartments/Pages/Technology.aspx

  This website offers game templates for Notebook that you can download and use in your classroom. Also see the SMART Tips Wiki for game templates.

Global Connections

The interactive whiteboard can serve as an awesome portal to the rest of the world. Some ideas were previously discussed about taking virtual adventures to explore other places that students might not otherwise encounter. Here are a few other resources that you might consider exploring.

- http://www.skype.com/

Skype is a free download that allows you to connect with an individual or group of people down the hall, across town, or across the globe. Once you have downloaded Skype, set up an account, and found the person you will be calling, you are ready to interact. Skype allows you to have a text chat online, transfer files, and talk with voice and video. You need to have a webcam to take advantage of the video chat. For chatting with a classroom, it definitely adds to the experience if you can have a video call. Be sure to take into consideration different time zones before setting up a call. Skype is an inexpensive way to bring an author, expert, group of students, etc., to your classroom. Skype is a nice alternative if your school does not have its own video conferencing resources.

♦ http://earth.google.com/

Use Google Earth as a way to virtually transport students to a new country or city on the interactive whiteboard. Explore the geography, examine how the city is laid out, what the buildings look like, and more. The images and 3D views for some cities available in Google Earth will help students get a better feel for the city and be able to make comparisons to cities with which they are familiar. Using Google Earth before a Skype call is a cool way to virtually transport the students to the caller's location.

♦ www.epals.com

Epals is a way for students to exchange information and ideas with students in other schools around the world. Epals offers opportunities for students to engage in collaborative projects, practice other languages, and share with students in more than 200 countries. Students can use the interactive whiteboard to share what they learn through the e-mails, digital artifacts, and other resources they may receive from their Epals with their classmates.

Conclusion

The Internet offers many different existing resources that people from around the world have shared. At no other time have there been so many rich resources for educators to find and use. Although the sheer quantity of resources can be extremely overwhelming at times, the fact that we can access both human and nonhuman resources on the other side of the world at the click of a mouse and at such a speed is amazing. The interactive whiteboard can be your portal to help students understand and access these valuable resources.

4

Present and Model
Material

Idea 7: Create Presentational Materials

Know Your Content and Your Students

Before you begin to prepare lesson materials, think about the content you want to introduce and the students to whom you are presenting it. Even though the material is presentational in purpose, is there a way for you to involve the students more actively? Can you incorporate images, sounds, or a video clip or two? What colors appeal to the students? What size text will you need to use? How big should the images be? How much text and how many images should you put on any one page? How many colors on one page are too many? Do your students have any special needs? Where do you want the focus of your students to go? Of the tools and resources you have, which are the best ones to teach the information, concept, or process you want the students to understand?

Basic Skills for Working with Pages

Being able to move and manipulate the pages in Notebook is important in the lesson creation process. To add new pages, you can click on the icon in the main toolbar that looks like a sheet of paper with a green plus sign on it (Figure 4.1). You can move forward a page by clicking on the right-facing blue arrow in the main toolbar and likewise you can move back a page by selecting the left-facing blue arrow.

Figure 4.1. Adding and Moving Through Pages

You can also add and navigate through your pages by finding the Page Tab (Figure 4.2, page 54) on the right or left side of your screen, depending upon which side of the screen you have your tabs. You can identify it because the icon on the tab looks like a page. By default you have this view available. If it is not, click on the page tab and you will see all of the pages that you have created below. If you only have one, you can also create pages from this area. You can identify the page that is active in your workspace in the page tab area because it will have a blue outline just inside the page border. In the upper right-hand corner of that page you will see a down arrow. Click on it to review a new menu of options. The options list includes the following:

Figure 4.2. Page Tab and Active Page

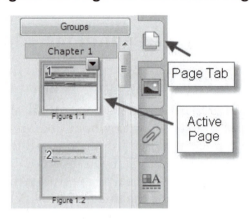

1. Delete Page, which deletes the page.

2. Clear Page, which clears all of the objects from the page, but will not clear the page background.

3. Insert Blank Page, which inserts a new blank page immediately after the active page.

4. Clone Page, which clones an exact replica of the active page. This feature is handy if you have created a page background you would like to apply to each page in your lesson. (However, if you plan to use the same background for many pages, you may want to look into creating a theme. How to create a theme is discussed later in this chapter.) It is also useful if you are using the pages to create a story and have the same background and characters that you would like to transfer to a new page.

5. Rename Page, which activates the text box below the page to allow you to change the name of the page to something other than the date stamp default. You can also double-click on the text box below the page to rename it.

6. Screen Shade, which applies a screen shade to the page that covers all objects on the page, much like a window shade. This can

also be applied using the Screen Shade icon from the main toolbar. The screen shade is useful when you would like to cover the whole page or even a part of it. Once the shade is on the page, you can click on one of the handles (circles) on the shade edge and drag the shade in the direction you would like it to go. This feature is a much more convenient than having to hold two sheets of paper over the overhead transparency.

7. Show All Links, which causes any object that has a link attached to it to flash. This can be particularly useful if you have attached a link to the object itself rather than to a corner icon attached to the object, as it will quickly identify which objects on your page are linked.

8. Add Page to the Gallery, which adds the active page to the Gallery. This is a great feature if you create a page that you would like to use again in the future. Once you add it to the Gallery, make sure to rename it so you can search for it more easily when you need it again. You will also need to remember to search for it in the My Content folder.

Moving Pages

Another thing that you can do that is not in the drop-down menu is rearrange the page order. You can move pages in the Groups menu, but you can also move them when working with the pages under the Page Tab. To move a page, click on it and then drag it to the new location where you would like it to go. You will know where it is going to move, as a blue line (Figure 4.3) appears in the desired location before the page actually moves.

Figure 4.3. Moving a Page

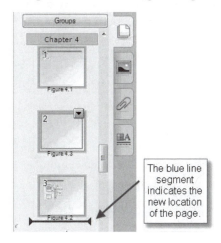

The blue line segment indicates the new location of the page.

Creating Different Types of Page Backgrounds

The blank page is a space for your creativity to come alive. There are various options for applying backgrounds to pages in Notebook including:

- ◆ Using one color
- ◆ Using two colors with a gradient
- ◆ Using a patterned background
- ◆ Inserting an image as the background
- ◆ Using a background from the Gallery
- ◆ Creating a theme background of your own

There are many different page background tools to help you create the page you are looking for.

Creating a Basic Page Background

One way to access the tools that allow you to change the page background is by right-clicking on the workspace of your Notebook page. When the drop-down menu appears, select Set Background. Doing so opens the Properties tab and provides you with options. Another way is by directly opening the Properties tab, making sure that you have not clicked on any objects on the page before doing so. By default, the Properties tab should open so you see the options in the Fill Effects menu (Figure 4.4). You will find that you have the same options available to you as you do to fill an object. You can have solid, gradient, pattern, and image fills for your page background. The image fill will not just fill the image in on the page once, but repeat the image various times to fill up the workspace.

Figure 4.4. Properties Tab and Fill Effects

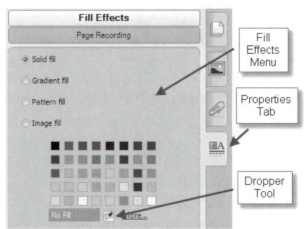

What type of background you choose is a matter of personal preference. It is a good idea to take into consideration the following:

♦ Is the color easy on the eyes? Is it too dark? To bright?

♦ Will the color distract from the content of the page?

♦ Will the background color clash with the text color and/or images you plan to use?

You may find that white backgrounds can be hard to look at over a period of time because of how bright they are. After some experimentation you may also find that some of the pastel shades tend to work well as they are softer colors. The gradient background color feature is nice as it can provide a subtler, smoother-looking background. Also, it is a good idea the first time you start working with page backgrounds to do so at your computer with your projector on. You may have a projector that is true to the color of what you see on your computer screen, but you may also have one that distorts the colors a bit from what you see. Take some time to play around with the colors in the palette. You can also choose More... and create some custom colors that the program will remember for you if you add them to your custom color palette found in the same menu.

Using the Dropper Tool

Another handy feature found in Fill Effects menu is the Dropper tool. This is one of my favorites. If you have an image on your page and you would like to match the page background to one of the colors in the image you can easily do so with the Dropper tool. First click on the Dropper tool and then click on the color that you would like it to pick up from the image (Figure 4.5). You will see that the color from the image is then applied to the page background. The Dropper tool can save a lot of time if you are trying to color match images and backgrounds. It will also work for matching text colors.

Figure 4.5. Using the Dropper Tool to Match Colors

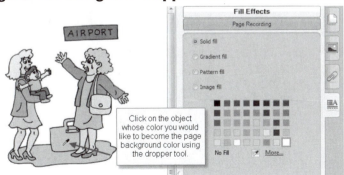

When designing pages for a lesson, the most important thing of course is the content. Afterwards, if you can find a related image and include it on the page it will make for a more attractive and interesting looking page. If you do use an image, you can find one image and let that determine the color scheme for the page. Using the Dropper tool to pull colors from the image will allow you to blend the page background and any other object colors on the page. Generally, a black text color goes well with most color schemes.

The Dropper tool will also work to custom match the color of your pen to your background, as this is necessary to create the magic eraser effect that is explained later in this chapter. Start by selecting the Pen tool from the main toolbar and choose one of the pen options from the drop-down menu. Click on the Properties tab and then the Line Style button to access the Dropper tool. You may first want to click on a thicker line style, if you do not already have one selected. Select the Dropper tool and then click on the page background color. Now your pen color and background color will be the same.

Using the Gallery to Find and Create Backgrounds

Start your search by opening the Gallery tab and then looking in the folder entitled Gallery Essentials. You can refresh your memory, if needed, of how to use the Gallery by referring to Chapter 2. When you click on the Gallery Essentials main folder, subfolders are revealed. Also in a lower window of that section you should see some topic bars that list the following (Figure 4.6):

- ◆ Pictures
- ◆ Interactive and Multimedia
- ◆ Notebook Files and Pages
- ◆ Backgrounds and Themes

Figure 4.6. Gallery Search Results

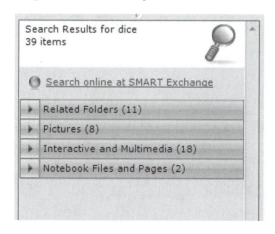

For building a page background, you will be most interested in the Notebook pages and the backgrounds and themes. The Notebook files referenced in the topics refer to full files, as you can also save a whole lesson file into the Gallery. If you are going to use a page from the Gallery it is best to put that background in first, before you add any text or objects. Pages work like paper over other objects and cover up anything that is already on the workspace. In contrast, you can insert a theme or background and it will automatically be placed behind any objects on the page. You can also change the page background color, gradient, pattern, or image fill at any time without having to worry about impacting the objects on the page.

Notebook Pages

To view the Notebook pages in the Gallery, click once on the triangle-shaped arrow that initially points to the right when you open the Gallery Essentials folder. The arrow will then point down and the pages in the Gallery will be revealed. The Notebook pages can be identified in the Gallery by a fold in the upper right-hand corner of the page (Figure 4.7). Remember that these need to be put on the workspace before any objects are added. Take a bit of time to see what pages are already prepared in the Gallery so the next time you are creating a lesson you have an idea of what is ready for you to use.

Figure 4.7. Notebook Pages

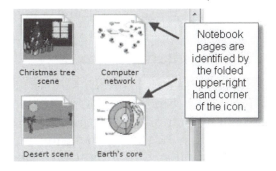

With each update of Notebook the content grows. Some examples of the content you will find on Notebook pages are:

- Story backgrounds like houses, schools, forests, and parks
- Traceable numbers and letters
- Math charts, grids and templates
- Outline maps
- Venn diagrams

- Calendars

- Representations of cycles and how things work

- Manuscript paper for writing music

- The Periodic Table of Elements

- Clock templates for time practice

To add the page to the workspace, double-click on the page or click and drag it onto the workspace. You can also click on the page you would like to use then click on the down arrow. From there choose, Insert in Notebook. The page will be automatically placed and you will not be able to move it. Although there may be images on the pages, you will not be able to move or edit them because they are a permanent part of the background. Many of the Notebook pages can have the page background color changed. To find out if you can do so for the page you are working with, right click on the workspace and choose Set Background, if the option is available. The Properties menu will open and you can make a choice about how you want the background to look.

To get rid of a page that you do not like, either delete it or add a new page over the top it from the Gallery to cover it up. Remember to label any pages you create and add to the Gallery and that when searching for pages you created, you need to search in My Content, rather than in Gallery Essentials. If you would like to close the Notebook pages and files area in the Gallery when you are searching, click once on the arrow and the content will be hidden until you want to open it again.

Page Backgrounds

Page backgrounds share features with pages, with the exception that they will automatically insert behind any objects that are already on the workspace. They will be automatically placed and cannot be moved. You will find the most page backgrounds by opening up the Gallery Essentials folder. Click on the arrow pointing to the right once and the page backgrounds and themes will be made available. You will be able to identify the page backgrounds because they have an upturned corner of the page in the lower right-hand corner of the Gallery file.

Some of the backgrounds you will find in the Gallery have the following topics:

- Holiday

- Nature

- Handwriting practice paper

- Math grids and graphing paper
- Lined borders
- Classroom
- Professional for presentations

Inserting a page background follows the same process as inserting pages and objects from the Gallery. Make sure to be on the page to which you would like the background to be applied. Adding a new page background to the same page covers up the old one. If you have a background you would like to use on multiple pages, don't forget to clone it before adding the rest of your page content to make the most of your time. If you would like to add the same background to multiple pages, you may want to consider using an existing or creating your own theme.

Themes: Using Existing Themes

Themes are found in the same area as page backgrounds. You can identify a theme because it does not have any upturned corners (Figure 4.8). Themes are set up with the idea that each of your pages in a group or entire Notebook file can use the same theme throughout.

Figure 4.8. Backgrounds and Themes

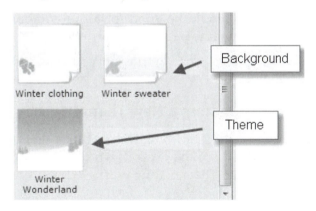

When you go to add a theme to your workspace, a pop-up window will appear and you will be asked if you want to:

Insert theme on all pages

Insert theme on all pages of current group

Insert theme on current page only

You can insert the theme the same way you insert any page, background or image from the Gallery. Some common themes in the Gallery Essentials folder are:

♦ School

♦ Nature

♦ Holidays

♦ Presentational

The themes may look similar to the pages and page backgrounds, but they are distinct in that you can edit them. You can also create your own theme that will then act as a template, having no objects that will move, as they just become part of the theme page.

When deciding whether or not to create a theme, it will be more worthwhile if it is going to be something that you want to easily apply to multiple pages in a Notebook file or want available for multiple lessons. In most cases, you can achieve the same look on a page with a theme as you can by creating a page and then adding it to the Gallery. Benefits of using the theme are:

♦ All objects on the page are automatically locked in place and immobile.

♦ Themes can be applied to all pages in a group or in the whole file automatically. This would be good for a presentation in which you want to use the same page for consistency.

♦ The font will stay consistent with what you selected when you created the theme.

Creating a New Theme

To create your own theme, start by having a blank workspace. From the main menu, select Format. From the drop-down menu, select Themes. From the next menu select Create Theme. Your workspace will now be ready to make your new theme.

1. In the text box entitled Theme name (Figure 4.9), name your theme as you would like it to appear in the My Content folder.

2. Add objects from the main toolbar or images from the Gallery to your workspace.

3. Right-click in the workspace area to set the page background color or style.

Figure 4.9. Creating a Theme

4. Double-click on the text box that says Theme Text Style. Highlight those terms. Then from your text box options select the font size, style, and color you would like to have be the default font for the page. Click on the page somewhere outside of the text box to exit the text box.

5. Choose Save.

6. Once you save, you will see the page move into the My Content area. From there you can add it to a blank page in your Notebook file. Decide if you want to insert it on all pages, in a particular group of pages or on just one page.

7. Click on the text box icon in the main toolbar to activate the text box and then click on the page. You do not need to select one of your default text options from the drop-down menu because you already set a default font when you created the theme page.

8. Click anywhere on the page and begin typing. The text you type will be the default that you chose when you set the theme.

Creating a New Theme from an Existing Page

Another option is to create a theme from an existing page. This option allows you to turn any page you have created into a theme page. It also allows you to make use of any Notebook pages or backgrounds from the Gallery Essentials that you are not able to use when you use the Create Theme option.

Begin by having the page background and any objects or text on the page from which you will create the new theme.

Then, open the Format menu, select Theme and then choose Create Theme from Page. When you do so, the background and content from the page you created the theme on, will be transferred into the theme editing page and you can make any further adjustments you like, following the same steps as you would for the Create Theme option (Figure 4.10). Remember not to confuse your original page background with the newly created theme. Your theme will be added to the My Content folder and you will need to add it to a new blank page. What you will see immediately after the theme is created in your workspace will still be your original page from which the theme was created.

Figure 4.10. Making a Theme from an Existing Background

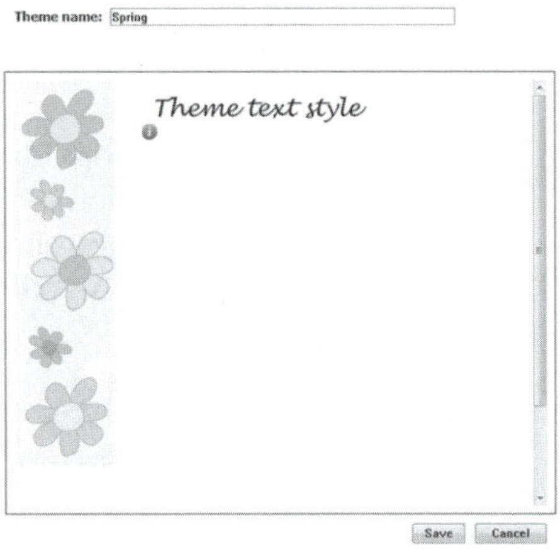

Editing and Saving Existing Themes

To edit an existing theme from the Gallery Essentials folder or one of your own, click on the theme you would like to edit in the Gallery. Then click on the down arrow and choose Edit Theme from the list of options. The theme will be added to a Notebook page and be ready to edit. Use the same process you used to create a new theme.

General Considerations When Working with Text

Generally speaking, when creating instructional material with any interactive whiteboard software, avoid using font sizes smaller than 28 points. A good standard size to use is 36 points. You want to make the information easy to read for all students, including those in the back row. If you have students with visual impairments you will likely want to use a larger font, make sure they are seated in the front, and provide a paper copy of your presentation materials to them to have at their desk. Another thing to consider is making sure to choose fonts that are easy to read. There are many fun and fancy fonts available; those are best used sparingly. Reserve them for titles on pages or something you want to accent or highlight. Using too many fonts on a page can be distracting as well. It may be a good idea to pick a font that you want to use as your standard font and stay with it in most cases. Use the font color, size, and style to your advantage to draw students' attention where you would like it to go.

Another consideration when working with text is how you will display it on a page and how much text you will put on any one page. Putting too much text on a page can be counterproductive, as it may clutter the space and confuse students as to where the important content is. Trying to fit too much on a page may also force you to use a smaller font size than what is optimal for students to be able to see. When in doubt, it is likely better to just create another page and split up the content.

Basic Skills for Working with Text and Objects

There likely will be times when you will want to hide text so students will not immediately see an answer to a question. There are various ways to hide text using the Notebook tools. The following are some basic skills you will need in order to use all of the text-hiding features explained in this chapter:

- ◆ Locking
- ◆ Grouping
- ◆ Customizing and Filling Objects
- ◆ Cloning
- ◆ Ordering Objects and Text
- ◆ Aligning Objects and Text

These skills are explained first and then followed by explanations of the various ways to hide text.

Locking

Once you have the text in place on your page where you want it to be, you will want to lock it in place. You will want to lock objects in place because when students come to the board to interact with the information, any text or objects that are not locked in place will be mobile. To lock the text in place, right-click on the text and from the drop-down menu that appears, select Locking. Notice that there is a shortcut command (Ctrl+K for PCs and Ctrl+L for Macs) for locking. You are likely to use the locking feature frequently, so it may be handy to learn the shortcut for locking text in place.

The Locking menu has four options:

♦ Unlock: If you have locked an object and need to unlock it you will need the first option to do so. It also has a shortcut.

♦ Lock in Place: This locks the object and allows no movement of it whatsoever.

♦ Allow Move: This locks the shape of the object to maintain its integrity, but allows the object to be moved up and down on the page. It will not allow the object to be rotated.

♦ Allow Move and Rotate: This feature also locks the shape of the object so it cannot be adjusted. It allows the object to be moved on the page and rotated. Clicking once on the object reveals a green handle (circle) at the top of the object. Clicking on the handle and moving the mouse in the direction you would like the object to move rotates it.

When working with text that you want to stay in the same place on the page, you will want to choose Lock in Place.

Grouping and Ungrouping

If you have multiple text boxes on your page that you need to lock down, you may want to consider grouping them before you lock them. This will save you time if you have to come back and edit the text later. There are two options to group objects. These directions apply to any object (e.g., text, clip art, shape, line, photo, and inserted image).

♦ *Option 1:* To group, you can use a marquis select (Figure 4.11) or click on text boxes individually. To do a marquis select, move your mouse pointer to the upper left hand corner of the workspace. Click and drag over the top of all of the text boxes you would like to group together. If done correctly you will notice that all of the text boxes have dashed blue lines around them. Now, click on the down arrow of any of the text boxes and select Grouping. In the next menu that appears, choose Group. An alternative to using the down arrow is directly using the shortcut Ctrl+G.

♦ *Option 2:* If you prefer not to use the marquis select, or if it is a case in which you do not want all of the objects on the page to be grouped together, you can hold down the Ctrl key and then click on each individual object that you would like to be part of the group. You can follow the previous grouping instructions or you can also right-click on any of the active objects to display the options menu. Select Grouping and then Group or use the shortcut Ctrl+G.

Figure 4.11. Marquis Select

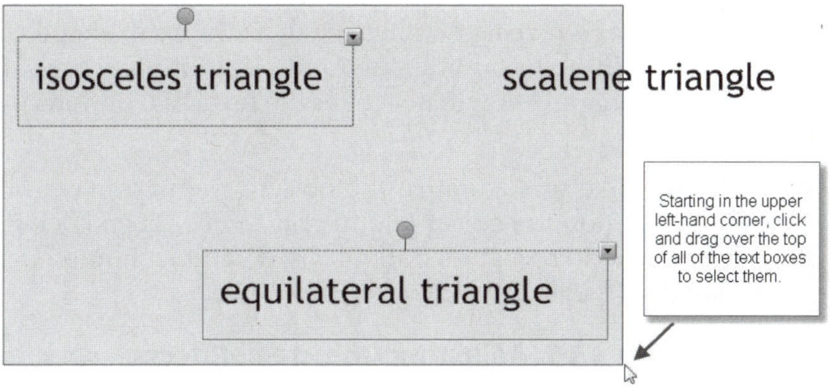

isosceles triangle

scalene triangle

equilateral triangle

Starting in the upper left-hand corner, click and drag over the top of all of the text boxes to select them.

Now that the objects are grouped, you can use the locking shortcut or the locking option from the menu and lock all of objects together. This process will save you from having to individually lock each text box should you need to do future editing as you will only need two steps to unlock any objects you have grouped together and locked.

At some point, you may need to ungroup your objects. To do so, there are two options:

♦ *Option 1:* Click on the grouped objects to activate them on the workspace. Then select the down arrow. In the new menu that appears, select Grouping and then from the sub menu, select Ungroup. You can also right-click on the activated grouped objects and get the same drop-down menu options. You will now be able to do any necessary editing.

♦ *Option 2:* Click on the grouped objects to activate them on the workspace. Press the keyboard shortcut Ctrl+R and your objects will be ungrouped.

Customizing and Filling Objects

To hide text with a shape, you first need to select the shape you want to use from the main toolbar by finding the shape icon represented by an orange square and a blue circle (Figure 4.12, page 68).

Figure 4.12. Creating Shapes

Clicking on the shape reveals another menu with many shape choices. Initially, the shapes will be in outline only and will not have any fill. You need to add fill to the shape or it will not cover the text. Two options for adding fill are the following:

♦ If you would like to customize the object to always have fill, start by clicking on the object you intend to use. Then click on the Properties tab to reveal fill options. By default it should open to display the Fill Effects window (Figure 4.13).

Figure 4.13. Adjusting Object Fill Effects

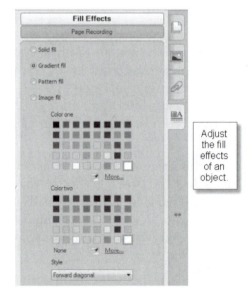

♦ There are four options for fill (see Figure 4.13).

• Solid Fill: The object will be filled with one color. Select the color you like from the color choices in the menu.

• Gradient Fill: The object will be filled with two colors of your choice. You can also choose the direction of the gradient.

• Pattern Fill: The object will be filled with a pattern.

- Image Fill: The object will be filled with an image. You will need to have an image saved as a file to use this option. An alternative is to directly use an image from the Gallery or your own source that you can drag onto the Notebook page.

Once you have chosen the fill style, you also have the option to change the line style. Below the Fill Effects button you will find one called Line Style (Figure 4.14).

Figure 4.14. Creating and Customizing Lines

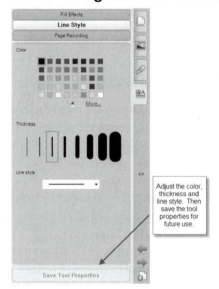

Select the Line Style button to reveal your options. You can change the color, as well as the thickness and style of the line. Although there is an Object Transparency feature that works great with Venn diagrams and in other circumstances, you will not want to use that here as it will make your object partially transparent, revealing the text below that you are trying to hide. Once you have made your selections, finish the customization process by clicking on Save Tool Properties at the bottom of the window (see Figure 4.14). The next time you click on the shape icon in the main toolbar you will find that it has the properties you chose in the customization process. You can also customize lines the same way you customize shapes.

When you move your mouse back into your work area after saving the properties, you will see a crosshair cursor (Figure 4.15, page 70). This means that the object tool is activated and at the next click and drag of your mouse you will create the object that you just designed in the workspace.

Figure 4.15. Object with Active Crosshair Cursor

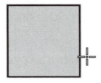

Make as many objects as you would like and then click on the Select icon in the main toolbar to return to a regular mouse function and turn off the object creation function. If you do not click on the Select icon, you will continue to make objects.

Filling Objects Without Customizing

There may be times that you do not want to customize the object because you only plan to use it once. If you do not want to customize, you can use the following process.

Click on the Object icon in the main toolbar and select the object you would like to use. When you move the mouse into the workspace you will see the crosshair cursor, indicating that the next click and drag will create an object. Create an object and then click on the Select icon in the main toolbar to deactivate the object creation function.

You now need to add fill to your object if you are going to use it to cover text. Right-click on the object and choose Properties from the drop-down menu. This will open the Properties tab. You can also access the Properties area by clicking directly on the Properties tab; just make sure that your object stays active. Choose your fill effects and your line effects in the same manner you did in the customization process above. Any fill or line changes you make are immediately applied to the object. Change the colors and styles as many times as you would like, until you get the effect you are looking for. Your object should still be active, so when you are done making your color and style selections click on the object and move it to the desired location.

Cloning

If you would like to create more than one of the same object, you can use the clone feature. When you right-click on the object, choose Clone from the drop-down menu. You can save a step by clicking on the object and using the shortcut Ctrl+D. Clone as many times as you like.

Infinite Cloner

Should you ever need an object or text that will keep cloning itself, try the Infinite Cloner feature. To find this feature, right-click on the object you would like to clone and from the drop-down menu, select Infinite Cloner. This will create an object that when you click on it once rather than becoming active and moving, it will create an infinite number of clones of itself that you can drag to a new location. If you need to edit the infinite cloner object, click on it once and then click on the Infinite Cloner symbol where the drop-down arrow usually is. Click on the phrase Infinite Cloner that appears and the object will return to functioning as a normal object. A secondary way to accomplish the same process is by right-clicking on the object and then clicking on the phrase Infinite Cloner when it appears.

The following are some ideas to get you started thinking about how you might use the Infinite Cloner feature in your own content area:

♦ If you are doing a reading comprehension activity with younger children or want the activity to go more quickly, you may create an Infinite Cloner for each of the words true and false. That way students can drag the answer to the blank.

♦ For counting practice, you could add different images to the page and ask students to add a specific number of each of the objects to the page. For example, you could use the farm background scene from the Gallery and ask students to add 10 cows, 5 turkeys, and 7 ducks to the farm. From there you could extend the activity to ask students questions about the scene they created, asking them to remove animals to help with subtraction practice and more.

♦ For world languages, when students learn to conjugate, the verb endings could be infinitely cloned. Students could be asked to add the correct ending to the verb stem when provided with the corresponding subject pronoun.

♦ For a unit on weather, one of the map backgrounds in the Gallery could be used along with the weather symbols also found in the Gallery. The different weather symbols could be set up as Infinite Cloners so students could hear or read a weather report and have to place the weather in the correct location on the map. This could also be used to practice geography and also would make another good activity for a world language classroom.

Ordering Objects and Text

You will find that having an understanding of the ordering feature is important if you want to:

♦ Understand why when you add a new object to the page, it keeps covering up other objects.

- Show a question on your interactive whiteboard and have the answer hidden on the page. You can type the question so it is visible and then hide the answer under a shape or other object. To reveal the answer, just click and drag the object that is on top of the text and the answer will be displayed.

- Create an object that has multiple layers. You may want to have text stand out on the page. One way to do this is to create one or more shapes and then add the text on top of it and group the objects together.

- Understanding ordering is also important when you start hiding objects on the page using effects like the magic eraser and the magnifier, both tools being explained later in this chapter.

To make full use of grouping objects, you also need to know how to order them. You can order objects and then group them together to give them more depth. When grouping a text box with a shape, you will likely want to see the text. To do so you will need to know how to order the text box so it appears on top of the object or you will not be able to read the information. When you add objects and text boxes to a page, it is important to remember that whatever object you put on the page first is ordered to the bottom by default. It is kind of like adding papers to a stack of paper; the newest will go on top, unless you make a change to the order and send it further to the back.

If as you are working you find that you would like to move an object or text box further to the back or bring it to the front there are features that will allow you to do that. Start by right-clicking on the object that you would like to move to bring up the options menu and then select Order (Figure 4.16). You will see the following options in the next menu that appears:

- Bring to Front (PC shortcut: Ctrl+Shift+PgUp)

  Brings object to the very front of the group of objects.

- Send to Back (PC shortcut: Ctrl+Shift+PgDn)

  Sends object to the very back of the group of objects.

- Bring Forward (PC shortcut: Ctrl+PgUp)

  Brings object forward, one object or layer at a time.

- Send Backward (PC shortcut: Ctrl+PgDn)

  Sends object backward, one object or layer at a time.

Depending upon the object that you are planning to order, some of the options may be grayed out. For instance, if you are planning to change the order of an object that is already at the very front, it will not let you bring it to

Figure 4.16. Ordering Objects

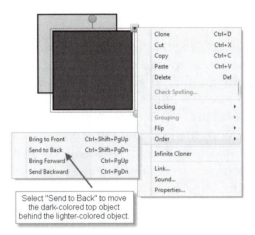

the front or bring it forward. Choose where you would like to send the object in the order and select that option. You will see the object move on the page.

Aligning Objects and Text

There will be text and other objects that you will want to be able to line up to improve the overall appearance of the page. The Alignment tool found in the main menu allows you to do so. From the drop-down options in the View menu, select Alignment. A new window will pop up with the following options:

♦ Show guides for active objects: This will show you a guide so you can line up objects with one another on the page.

♦ Show vertical page center guide: This will provide a vertical guide down the center of the page.

♦ Show horizontal page center guide: This will provide a horizontal guide through the middle of the page.

♦ Snap objects to guides: This will align the objects on your page to the guides.

♦ Guide colors: The default guide color is gray. If you would like to use a different guide color, select the gray box and a new menu of colors will pop up. Select the color you would like and choose OK.

Showing the vertical page center guide splits your page in half vertically. This can be beneficial if you are trying to divide objects on the page equally on each half. The same is true for the horizontal page center guide. If you use both the vertical and the horizontal guides together, it will allow you to divide the page into four equal quadrants so you can make sure your objects are equally distributed. If you select to show the guides for active objects, you must move the objects for the line guides to show. You can use the line like a ruler to help you line up any side of two or more objects so they are exactly in line with one another. It will also show a line down the center of each object when the two object centers are lined up with one another. Additionally, the horizontal and vertical centers will show up when the object is aligned or centered with them. Choosing the snap objects to guides option effectively snaps the objects to the line as it sounds like from the descriptor. For this option to work, you must also have selected to show the guides for active objects. Snapping the objects to a guide is useful if you have individual text boxes that you want to be in a straight line. You might use that for a sentence restructuring activity where the sentence is out of order and needs to be put back together. You can also use it with objects that cover up text in a hide and reveal type activity if you have multiple in a row and want to make sure the objects line up the same with the one next to or above it.

Ways to Use Text on a Page

Text Display on the Page

Sometimes you will want students to see all text on a page right away. This is the simplest use of text. Using what you learned in Chapter 1, you can create a text box and type the information that you would like displayed on the page. Making sure the text box is not active (you are no longer typing in it and it is ready to move like an object), you can then click on it once and move it to the desired location. Double clicking on the text box allows you to edit the text. Remember that to make font style or size changes you need to first highlight the text for the change to be applied. You can also use your mouse to access a Pen tool from the main toolbar to write or go to the interactive whiteboard to use a pen from the tray for handwritten text.

Customizing Your Text Tool

You can customize your text tool by clicking on the Text icon in the main toolbar. Once the drop-down menu appears, click on one of the fonts that you would like to replace with a different one and then click on the Properties tab at the right (Figure 4.17).

Figure 4.17. Customizing Text

Click on the Text Style button and select the font of your choice from the drop-down menu. Also choose the desired font size from the drop-down menu. You also have the option to make style choices like bold, italics, and underline. If you would like to change the color of the text, click on the Line Style button. From the new menu, choose the color of your choice. You can click on More… to customize your color even further. When you have made your selections, click on the Save Tool Properties button located in the bottom right-hand side of the of the Notebook file. The next time you use the text feature, you will notice that the default text style you modified has been changed.

Hiding and Revealing Text

Now that you have an understanding of the previously described skills, you are ready to start working with the numerous ways that you can hide text. In this section, you will learn how to do the following:

♦ Hide text with pull tabs

♦ Hide text with images

♦ Hide text with shapes

♦ Reveal text with animated objects

♦ Click and reveal Gallery tools

♦ Reveal text with the Magic Eraser

♦ Reveal text with the Magnifier tool

Hiding Text with Pull Tabs

Pull tabs are helpful in that they let you hide text or objects off the page. You can use them to keep the page from looking too cluttered, to hide questions and answers off the side of the page, and even to hide objects. You can reveal the information by pulling the tab onto the page and then pushing the information back off to the side when you are done if you want to remove the excess information. You can either use preexisting pull tabs in the Gallery or create your own.

There are multiple ways that a pull tab might be useful to you. Consider the following ideas on how to use pull tabs:

- Provide a question on your Notebook page for students to answer. The pull tab will have the answer to the question. Conversely, you can provide a statement on the page and the pull tab can reveal the question.

- Identify what x is in an equation.

- Provide an answer to a fill-in-the-blank question that is missing a word to complete a sentence.

- Show a picture and ask what is missing from the scene using the pull tab to reveal the answer(s).

- Show a solution to a problem and ask what step is missing.

- Show the image of an engine on your page, identify parts of it, and then pull a separate tab to each location to check answers.

- Show a picture or image on the screen and ask students to identify it or answer a question about it. The answer can be revealed with the pull tab.

- Provide a question on your Notebook page that has a pictorial answer or answers. Show different answers grouped together in one pull tab or attach one answer per pull tab, making various tabs.

- When giving notes for a class you can hide some or all of them off the side of the page to keep students' focus on only the information being explained.

- Reveal a sound for students to guess, repeat, or associate with a picture.

Finding Existing Pull Tabs

Doing a search in the Gallery for *Pull Tab* (searches are usually better when conducted in the singular rather than plural form of the word) locate the precreated tabs available in the Notebook software. Select the one and drag it onto the workspace or double-click the object to have it appear in the workspace. Once you place the pull tab on the page you will see prewritten instructions from SMART on how to use it. You may also be interested in checking out the folder in the Gallery entitled Layering. This folder contains sample pages from SMART with ideas on how to use pull tabs and other tools related to layering objects and text.

Creating Custom Pull Tabs

You can also create your own custom pull tabs. To do so you need to know how to create a text box and move and group objects. What is fun about making your own pull tabs is that you can be creative in doing so. Any object or image can act as the tab. You can use a basic arrow shape that points in the direction you want the text or object that is hidden off screen to be pulled so that it is revealed, or try other shapes, images, or text. To create an arrow-shaped pull tab (Figure 4.18), choose the arrow from your Shapes menu. Add it to the page and adjust it to the size you would like. You can fill the arrow shape with the color of your choice and change the line color and style. Add a direction for students using a text box that you place on top of the arrow shape. The simplest direction may be to just type "Pull." Place the text on top of the arrow shape and group the text and object together. Remember that you will want to first add the shape to the page and then the text. If you don't and the object is covering the text, you will just need to just adjust the order of the object to move the text to the front. Once you make your pull tab, it is a good idea to add it to the Gallery right away so you can use it in future lessons. Don't forget to rename it as well so you can easily find it in a search next time you need to use it.

Figure 4.18. Making a Pull Tab

To make this pull tab , use the arrow shape tool. Then, use a text box to type "Pull." Lastly, group the two objects together

Once you have created the pull tab, you will need to type the text that you are going to hide off-screen. Align the text next to the pull tab the way you would like it to be and then group the pull tab and the text together. Once they are grouped, drag the tab to the edge of the page until the text is hidden off the workspace. You will want to pull the text back on to the page to see if it lines up the way you would like. Using the same principles, you can also show one or more images, rather than having text as the hidden information that is pulled back onto the screen. You can also make the pull tab itself from a combination of a picture or clip art and the text (Figure 4.19). Note that in the figures that follow, the pull tab and the text and/or images that would be hidden off-screen are shown as part of the examples.

Figure 4.19. Lion Pull Tab

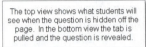

Name 5 mammals you can find at the zoo.

Another way to use the pull tab is to use an image as the tab in conjunction with a scene. If you are telling a story or have a picture theme on your page you can place objects (animals, people, things) on the page that when pulled display a question to answer, a response to a question, a direction or a comment (Figures 4.20 and 4.21). When you group objects this way, you will want to leave more space between the image serving as the pull tab and the text so the text is not visible on the screen. Creating a scene with multiple directions or questions can make the page more interactive and interesting (Figure 4.22).

Figure 4.20. Beaker Pull Tab

Figure 4.21. Counting Pull Tab

Figure 4.22. Creating a Scene with Pull Tabs

Hiding Text with Images

To begin, make sure that you have text on the page that is locked down and ready to be hidden. If you would like to hide the text with an image, open the Gallery tab at the right. Once open, you can search for a particular image by using the search box at the top right. Once you have found an image you want to use, there are three ways you can add it to your workspace:

1. Double-click on it;

2. Drag it onto the page; or

3. Click on it once and click on the down arrow. From the drop-down menu, select Insert in Notebook.

If you do not find what you are looking for in the Gallery, you may want to use other resources you have for images, or refer to Chapter 2 where finding images from other sources is discussed.

To hide the text, click on the image and move it until it covers the selected text you would like hidden (Figure 4.23). Because the image is the last thing you put on the page, it will automatically cover the text. If the image size needs to be adjusted, click on it once and make sure that it is active. You will know the object is active when you see the dashed blue lines around the edge and the green and gray handles. If you need to rotate the image, use the green handle to do so. Clicking on the handle and moving your mouse in the direction you would like it to turn will rotate it. If you need to enlarge the image, click on the gray handle and drag the image towards the bottom right-hand corner. To shrink it, drag the image towards the upper left-hand corner. Move the object to the final location and you will have successfully hidden the text.

Figure 4.23. Hide and Reveal Text with an Image

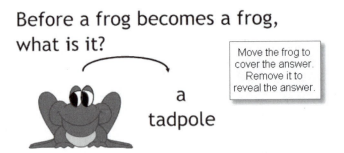

In addition to other sources of images previously discussed, you can also create your own image using the Screen Capture tool. You may find a portion of a picture or scene within or outside of Notebook that you would like to use as an image to hide text. Capture the image or portion of it that you want to use. Copy it from the page it captures to onto your workspace. Drag it so it covers the text you would like to hide. If you have more than one thing you would like to hide on the page, you could use multiple screen shots from the same image. After students answer all of the questions, they can put the pieces of the image back together as if it were a puzzle. The Screen Capture tool is a very versatile tool. To review how to use the Screen Capture tool, refer to Chapter 1.

Hiding Text and Other Objects with Shapes

You can also use shapes to hide text or any other type of object (Figure 4.24). To begin, start with your text locked in place on the page where you would like it to be. Then, choose the shape you would like to use from the main toolbar. Drag the shape over the top of the text and make any needed adjustments to the size, fill color, and line style by right-clicking on the shape, choosing Properties from the drop-down menu, and making any modifications. Repeat the process if you have more text to cover and would like to use different shapes or styles.

Figure. 4.24 Hide and Reveal Text with a Shape

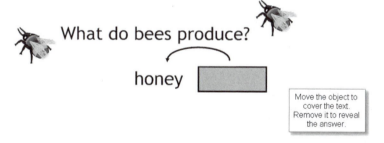

For a different look, you can group more than one object together, using the ordering tool to get the desired effect. Also, as an alternative, you may choose to start by putting a shape on the page, followed by text on top. These two objects can be grouped and locked. On top you can place another object offset so you can still see a portion of the bottom shape to give a look of more depth. The bottom shape should be at least a little bit bigger than the top. You can add more contrast by using a different color for each object. To reveal the text, click on the top shape and drag it off to the side. You can also click on the shape and delete it.

Creating Custom Shapes

You can create a custom shape by using the Shape Tool found in the main toolbar. You can identify this tool because it has a pen and a square in the icon (Figure 4.25). Click on the icon and it will activate the Shape Tool pen. Draw as you would with a regular pen, but create a shape. Make sure to connect your last line to a part of the shape. When you finish, the Shape Tool pen will straighten out the lines you drew. If you draw a shape like a square, rectangle, triangle, or circle, the tool will smooth out the lines of your object. If the shape is irregular, the tool will straighten out the lines you drew as best as possible. You can fill the custom shape in the same way that you fill any other object.

Figure 4.25. Shape Tool

Revealing Text with Animated Objects

Start with your text on your page locked in the location you would like it to stay. Next, choose either a shape or an image to cover the text. Place the object of your choice on the page and cover the text with it. The first step in adding animation is to right-click on the object and choose Properties. From your options, choose Object Animation and a new menu of options will appear (Figure 4.26). Your first choices are in the drop-down menu labeled Types.

Figure 4.26. Object Animation

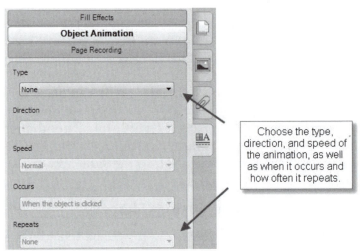

The following options appear in the Types menu:

♦ Fade In: Object will appear on the page from an originally invisible state.

♦ Fade Out: Object will fade away, becoming transparent and revealing what is underneath.

♦ Flip Around Axis: Object will flip around a center axis.

♦ Fly In: Object will fly in from outside the page.

♦ Fly Out: Object will fly off the page.

♦ Shrink and Grow: The first time the object is clicked it will grow and the next time it will shrink.

♦ Spin: Object will spin around.

You will want to take a little time and play with the different options, as you will likely find a few favorites. Some will work well for revealing answers and others will work better for other purposes. As you try each one out, the action will be immediately applied to the object so you can see how each type of object reacts. You will also have the option to choose the speed at which you would like the animation to occur. Your options are slow, normal, and fast. You can also choose whether you want the object animation to occur when you enter the page or when you click on the object. In the instances when you are revealing objects, you will want to select "when you click on the object." The enter the page option works well if you are presenting some notes and would like the text or something else to fly in from the side and get the attention of your students. Additionally, you have the option to choose how many times the animation will repeat, with options ranging from none to forever. The options Flip Around Axis, Fly In, Fly Out, and Spin in the Types list above also have the option of choosing a direction. You can have the object spin clockwise or counterclockwise, fly in or out from the left, right, top, bottom, etc., and you can have the object flip around its axis from the middle or the different edges. Once you have made your selection, the animation will automatically be applied to the object.

Animations can be great tools for varying the way information is revealed and presented. However, they seem to be best used in moderation. Keep in mind where you want the attention of your students to go. If you have an animation on the page that is spinning forever, it is likely to turn into a distraction rather than a quick attention-getter. The same thing can be said for animated clip art that you may find.

Animation tip: If you use the animation type that fades out or it seems that your animated object has disappeared, clicking on a new page in your Notebook file and then returning to the page with the animations on it should restore the animation.

Revealing Text with Gallery Tools

Notebook also provides objects in the Gallery that are preset to reveal the answer underneath them. To use these, lock the text you would like to use in place and then go to the Gallery and open the Lesson Activity Toolkit folder. From there, open the Tools subfolder. In that folder you will find various shapes of Click and Reveal tools (Figure 4.27, page 84).

Figure 4.27. Click and Reveal Tools in the Gallery

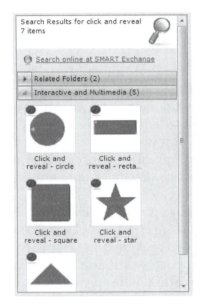

You can also search for these tools in the Gallery using the term *click and reveal* and you will find them under Interactive and Multimedia. Choose the one you would like and drag it onto the workspace and cover the text with it. Click the click-and-reveal tool once to reveal the answer underneath it. Click it again to hide the text. If you do not like the standard color that it comes in, you can edit the color by clicking on the double arrow in the upper left-hand corner of the shape (Figure 4.28). Click on the color square that you see and a new menu of colors will pop up. Select the color of your choice and then choose OK. Your click-and-reveal tool will have the new color that you selected. If you plan to use that particular color of the click-and-reveal tool, you may want to add it to your My Content folder so it is always ready for use without needing to modify the color. Don't forget to label it so you can easily find it again.

Figure 4.28. Editing a Click and Reveal Object

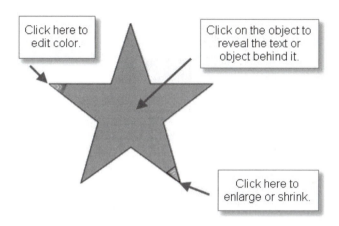

If you would like to have multiple click-and-reveal tools that are the same shape and color, you may want to use the clone feature. Right click on the tool and select Clone. Clone as many times as you would like. When you right-click on the tool you will find that you have other options that include Cut, Copy, Paste, Delete, Flash, Order, Locking, and Link. Also on this tool you will see four dots in the lower right-hand area of it. Click and drag the object toward the bottom right-hand corner of the workspace to enlarge the tool and drag toward the top left to shrink it. In addition to using this tool to reveal answers, you may also like to try it for a concentration game.

Another click-and-reveal tool is the Balloon Pop (Figure 4.29, page 86). You will find this tool in the same area as the other click and reveal tools. There are a few main differences with this tool. When you click on the double arrow, instead of having the ability to change the color, you can type on the side of the balloon that will be visible on the screen.

The balloon color changes are generated randomly as you drag different ones out of the Gallery. Another feature of the Balloon Pop is that when clicked it makes a popping sound. To enlarge the balloon, click on the triangle-shaped tab in the lower right-hand corner of the balloon and drag toward the bottom right of the page to enlarge and toward the upper left to shrink it. For variety and a bit of fun, students can also pop the balloon with a koosh ball by throwing it at the interactive whiteboard.

Figure 4.29. Balloon Pop

Revealing Text with the Magic Eraser

The Magic Eraser is a fun effect because when you use the standard eraser with this effect it seems as if the words on the screen are appearing out of nowhere (Figure 4.30). What is really happening is that you are erasing a layer of digital ink that you colored over the top of the text, using the same pen and background colors. To create this effect, start by adding the text you would like to hide to your workspace and lock it into place. The next step is to choose a page background color you would like to use and fill the page with that color. The last step is to select the pen tool from the main toolbar and make it the same color as the page background. The first time you try to create the Magic Eraser effect, you may want to try doing it using the white page background and a white pen.

Figure 4.30. Creating the Magic Eraser Effect

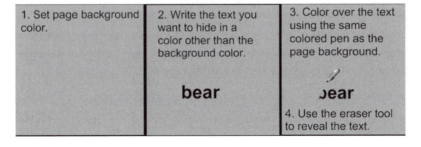

1. Set page background color.	2. Write the text you want to hide in a color other than the background color.	3. Color over the text using the same colored pen as the page background.
	bear	**ɔear**
		4. Use the eraser tool to reveal the text.

If you pick a nonstandard color, you will need to use the Dropper tool to match the pen to the page background color. You will want to adjust the pen so you have a line that is relatively thick. The last step is to draw over the text you would like to hide with the pen. The text will disappear. To reveal the text, use the Eraser tool as you normally would to erase the digital ink from the pen. The text will then be revealed. You can also use this same process to hide objects and other images.

Revealing Text with the Magnifier Effect

To use the magnifier effect, you will first need to have a Magnifier tool. This tool does not actually magnify any text, but it simulates the idea that the Magnifier tool is helping you to find hidden text (Figure 4.31). You can use many different things to create the Magnifier tool, but to illustrate the idea, start by searching in the Gallery for *magnifying glass*. Make sure you do not select the transparent one. Add the magnifying glass to your workspace.

Figure 4.31. Creating the Magnifier Effect

The magnifier effect allows you to hide text and find it with the tool by making use of colors and layers. To hide text you will need to make the page background and the text color the same. You can choose to lock the text down for this effect or not. If a student clicks on the spot on the page where the text is locked, however, it will give away the location of the hidden text. Once you have chosen the background color and changed the text color so it is the same as the background color and is hidden, you will want to test out the Magnifier tool. Because of how layers work, if the last thing you add to your workspace is the Magnifier tool, it will automatically cover up the text. If this is the case, you need to right click on the Magnifier tool you are using and select Order. From there, select Send to Back. Now, move the Magnifier tool over where the text on your page is and it will go behind the text and expose it. Check to make sure that any other text you have hidden also exposes itself with the Magnifier tool. You can create your own unique Magnifier tool with any object whose fill color contrasts enough with the color of your text to make it stand out or just use the magnifying glass from the Gallery.

If you right-click on the magnifying glass from the Gallery, you will see that you can ungroup the white center of the glass from the magnifier itself and change the fill color of the magnifying glass. When you are finished, regroup the center and the magnifying glass and you have a new magnifier. If you would like to use it again in the future, add it to your My Content folder.

Presenting a Lesson

When you are ready to present a lesson, there are a couple of tips you might find helpful. There are times when it is useful to present the lesson without view of or access to any of the side tabs. To view a presentation in full screen mode, click on the blue icon in the main toolbar that looks like a screen. To move through the different pages of the presentation, use the blue arrow pointing to the right to advance and the blue arrow pointing to the left to reverse. By clicking on the gray line with arrows on each end, more options will be shown in the toolbar. You will be able to add a new page, access the Select icon, undo actions, and access the magic pen. To access more tools in full screen mode, click on the More Options icon, represented by three dots (…). When you are done working in full screen mode, click on the blue full screen icon.

If you do not want to present in full-screen mode, use the Auto-Hide feature to enlarge your presentation space. This way you can also easily access any menus in the side tabs. When you have the page sorter tab active, you will see that the Auto-Hide selection box is located at the bottom left of that section. Select it by clicking on the box to the left of the Auto-Hide text to activate it. When you have the Auto-Hide feature active, you will find that when you click on the workspace area of Notebook, that any side tab you have open will be minimized so only the side tabs themselves are visible. If you are using a Mac computer, instead of using the Auto-Hide, you can pull the handle on the Page Sorter tab to minimize the size of the tab and increase your viewing area.

Conclusion

There are many ways to design pages to present material using tools available in the Notebook software. As always, it is essential to make the content of your creatively designed pages the center of the lesson and know what types of presentations will appeal to your students.

5

Provide Opportunities for Practice

Idea 8: Create Activities to Practice and Process

Considerations When Creating Activities

One of the more difficult tasks for teachers who are just starting to use an interactive whiteboard is figuring out how to use it. At first teachers tend to transfer what they have always done to the interactive whiteboard because they are not sure how else to use it. That is one reason why many of the whiteboard lessons you find online look like worksheets. While there is value in doing exercises from a worksheet on an interactive whiteboard to model, practice, discuss work, etc., that should not be the only way the board is utilized. As you begin to create your own activities, you may want to consider the following questions:

- How will you design the activities?

  - What types of skills should students have after completing the different activities?

  - How will you create the activities so they maximize student participation? What other resources can you use in conjunction with the interactive whiteboard to achieve this?

  - What types of tools are available in the Notebook software to help you design the activities? How will you use those tools to design activities that are both educationally valuable and interesting to students?

- What kinds of activities can you create?

Ensure Opportunities for Student Interaction with the Board

A potential danger of the interactive whiteboard is that it turns into a glorified projection tool. To avoid this, spend some time thinking about how you will make sure all students have an opportunity to interact with the material on the board. One way to increase student opportunities is to give as many opportunities as you can to the students to lead the activities at the board. Here are a few ideas on what students can do:

♦ Go over answers to practice activities with their classmates by revealing answers after the class has done the activity.

♦ Run the activities from the Lesson Activity Toolkit that is described in detail later in this chapter.

♦ Work out the answers to any questions or problems you are giving the class at the board while the rest of the class works at their seats.

♦ Direct most interactive Internet-based activities.

♦ Lead, guide, or take notes on a class discussion.

♦ Demonstrate or explain a process.

♦ Present and explain their work to the class.

♦ Examine and evaluate models of student or professional work.

Initially, you may be more inclined to direct most of the activities from the board while you develop a comfort level teaching with the interactive whiteboard. Over time you are likely to find that standing off to the side gives you more time to observe student participation in and comprehension of the activities. Being able to stand off to the side lets you direct most of your focus to observing the students.

To ensure students have fair opportunities to interact with and direct activities at the interactive whiteboard you will want to have some sort of system in place. The following are some ideas on how to offer students equal opportunities to come to the board.

♦ *Popsicle sticks:* Have students' names written on popsicle sticks or some other similar type of system. Have one cup or pocket per group of students to keep them in when they have not been called on recently and one for students who have recently been to the board.

♦ *Random Word Chooser:* Use the Random Word Chooser (Figure 5.1) from the Lesson Activity Toolkit in the Gallery. Click and drag it onto the page or double-click it to add it directly. At the bottom, choose the number of names you have in your class. In the bottom left-hand corner, click on the No Repeat box if you would like no names to be selected more than once. Then begin typing the names for each student in your class in the boxes. Make sure to save the file once you have typed in all of the names. Choose Select at the bottom of the activity to have it randomly choose a name. If you have more than one class, you can create a separate page in the same Notebook file for each class. Save time by cloning the page for as many classes as you need before you start typing in individual names. You can label the page names with the class hour to help you navigate between pages.

Figure 5.1. Random Word Chooser

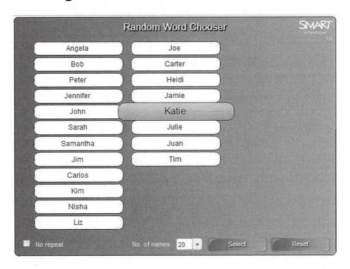

- *Spinner Tool:* You can also use the Spinner tool (Figure 5.2) from the Lesson Activity Toolkit in the Gallery. You can create up to twelve segments and can write in the names of your students in the text box for the segment. Most classes have more than twelve students so you could use more than one spinner. A limitation would be that you will not be able to keep track of who was last selected.

Figure 5.2. Spinner Name Selector

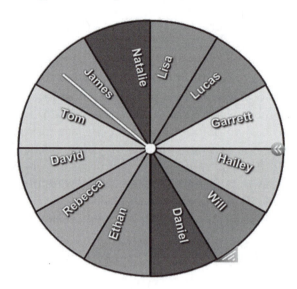

♦ *Random Name Generator:* Try out the website www.superteacher
tools.com, which offers online tools to choose names and groups.
Scroll down on their page and look for the Random Name Generator. Follow their directions to create a new class list. Once you
have created the list, you can embed the link for the website in
your Notebook file. Attach the link to an object or text that names
your class period if you have more than one. This site also offers
a random group generator and some interactive game templates.

Create Opportunities for Active Student Participation at Their Seats

Although an important part of participation is making sure all students
can interact with the board itself, what do you do when only one student can
touch the board at a time? This is the time when you ask yourself what other
resources you have in your room. It is essential to make sure that students at
their desks each have a way to interact with the lesson on the board. The following list of resources, which are explained in detail below, provide some
tools to use to involve students at their seats. The list takes into consideration
the varying resources that school districts may have available to them.

♦ Accompanying worksheets

♦ Paper

♦ Individual dry erase boards

♦ Laptops

♦ Hand-held mobile devices such as cell phones, iPod Touches, and the like

Accompanying Worksheets

Whereas using the interactive whiteboard as a tool to only project worksheets would not be a good use of it, you may find that a question or activity from a worksheet that is presented with more context, visual aids, or interactive support is useful. Rather than projecting the whole worksheet, take a few problems from it to practice and focus on. You might also use the worksheet along with a website to explore a topic as a class as a model or guided-learning experience. Students could be provided with a copy of the relevant questions on the worksheet.

It also may be very useful to project a worksheet that is a homework assignment or in-class activity that you want to explain with the visual support. You may want to model some part of what is expected so students better understand the task. You may also have an answer key to a homework assignment that you want students to quickly self-check at the beginning of the class period or that you want to review with them. A key element to remember is that you want students to have whatever the learning resource is in their hands as much as possible so they can directly interact with it. If you want them to do a worksheet because it has instructional value, then in most cases it is more valuable for them to have a copy of it in their hands to do themselves, rather than transferring it off the board.

Paper

Students can be asked to respond to a variety of things on an interactive whiteboard with pencil and paper. You may want students do a warm-up activity to review material or present a new challenge, an in-class practice activity to practice new material, or an exit activity to turn in to you to check their understanding of the day's material or to respond to other questions you have for them. You may also want a more extended written response to, for example, a writing prompt, a related image, a portion of an article on the Internet, a blog post, a video clip, or a math or science problem. Paper and pencil are still useful tools.

Individual Dry Erase Boards

Individual dry erase boards offer a bit more flexibility than pencil and paper, except if you want the students to create a longer response to something or if you will want them to turn in the response. Use the dry erase boards to have students provide responses to practice activities or come up with their own questions. A great benefit of the dry erase boards is that you can ask students to hold up their answers for you to assess if they comprehend the material and give them immediate feedback.

Hand-Held Devices

Cell phones and other hand-held devices that have mobile computing possibilities can also be used in tandem with an interactive whiteboard lesson. Here are a few examples:

- The website http://www.polleverywhere.com/ allows teachers to pose questions to their class and students can respond to those questions by texting in a response or by typing in a response from the website. When the teacher shows the questions on the board, students are provided with a code number to text or type that will then register immediately with the website and show the responses on the board for other students to see. Responses can be used to assess comprehension, generate in-class discussion, come up with questions for further inquiry about a topic, and more.

- The iPod Touch and devices like it can be used as part of a lesson as well. The teacher can introduce the lesson using the interactive whiteboard and then provide students with a resource on the Touch that allows them to individualize their practice. Students can then practice the skill at their own pace, repeating what they need to, and the teacher can move around the room to assist students. Some web-based practice sites, like www.quizlet.com, have applications for the Touch that allow more mobile practice. Quizlet is a site that allows students to review textual and visual material and provides flashcards, fill-in-the-blank questions, quizzes, and games. Instead of students doing vocabulary as a group, they can practice individually and advance at their own pace.

- Students can use mobile devices with the Internet to quickly access any information they need to find during a lesson. This allows less information to have to come directly from the teacher and more opportunities for students to engage in research and in finding their own answers.

- Mobile devices can also offer opportunities to individualize instruction. Students who need more practice can work at their own pace and students who need different learning opportunities can also access those. Many devices have recording capabilities which open up opportunities for students to record their voice and the voices of others for a multiplicity of purposes.

Laptops

Using laptops along with the interactive whiteboard, opens up a whole new dimension of possibilities. Some ways students might make use of a laptop in conjunction with the board include:

♦ Students have a copy of the Notebook software on their computer along with the lesson the teacher is presenting. The teacher can model any necessary elements of the lesson and students can do the practice activities on their own computer, while another student does it at the board. Students can work with more or less guidance from the teacher, depending upon the lesson set up and abilities of students. Students can access any links to other information from the lesson to practice concepts, explore and research.

♦ Students can explore answers to questions on the interactive whiteboard on their own computer. They can share them with one another via online resources like http://sync.in/ and http://www.scribblar.com/, which allow students to communicate in writing with one another in a space on the same website. Student conclusions can then be shared with the class by projecting the website on the interactive whiteboard.

♦ Students can also use the http://www.polleverywhere.com/ site from their computers to participate in the class by sharing information.

♦ Students can access web-based school subscriptions to information resources as well as the Internet to find answers to questions in the lesson, giving them a more active role in the class.

If your school has limited resources, avoid focusing on what you don't have and look at what you do. Dry erase boards can be very effective and fun for students and can be cut from shower board at building supply stores much less expensively than purchasing them individually from educational sources. Another key factor to remember as you choose your activities and practice tools is variety. If you use any tool exclusively every day students will likely get bored with it.

Using the Interactive Whiteboard as a Learning Station

For Small-Group Activities

In addition to a whole-group tool for instruction and practice, you can also use the interactive whiteboard as a learning and practice station. Some activities work great for whole-class instruction, whereas others are better for small group, pair, or individual practice. Many teachers have learning centers for their classrooms already; the interactive whiteboard can become another one. If you are not a teacher that tends to use learning centers as part of your instruction, the interactive whiteboard can turn into a station quite easily without having to create lots of other centers for students. When students are working independently on other work, you can have them take turns in small groups, pairs, or individually rotating through an activity on the interactive whiteboard that supports the learning objectives.

With the Recording Tool to Practice or Demonstrate a Process

You can also have students use the Recording tool (Figure 5.3) in Notebook to record a process and show their work as part of a portfolio. The recording can be done with or without audio, depending upon the resources that you have with your interactive whiteboard. If you do not have the ability to record voice with your board, you can just have students demonstrate a skill or process visually. You can demonstrate to your entire class how to use the tool before they come to the board to use it.

Figure 5.3. Page Recording

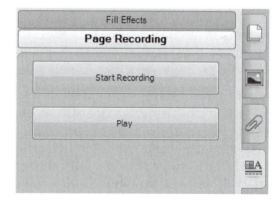

To find the Recording tool, make sure you are not clicked on any objects on the page and then click on the Properties tab. When you see the option called Page Recording, select it. Then choose Start Recording. Pick up your pen from the pen tray or use any of the other tools that you need to demonstrate the process. You will know that your actions are being recorded when you see the large red circle along with the abbreviation REC in the upper left-hand corner of your workspace. When you are done, select Stop Recording, which is found in the Page Recording area under Properties. To see the process you recorded, select Play from the same area or by using the on-screen tool-bar that appears in your workspace. Save the recording in the Notebook file the same way you would save any file. Choose Save in the File menu, name the file, and then save it to the location of your choice. Students can each save their own recording, demonstrating their skill or you can have each student create a separate page in the Notebook file, title the page with the student's name, and then show the process. Not only can students use this tool, but you can also use it to show any process and then save it for later presentation use. That way students can access it as part of a learning station if they need to see it more than once, or you might leave it for a substitute teacher who needs to present a lesson when you are absent.

Using the Interactive Tools and Activities from the Lesson Activity Toolkit to Preview, Practice, and Review

The Notebook software has many interactive tools included in the Lesson Activity Toolkit found in the Gallery. You should take some time to explore the available tools. The following material will give you an idea of the kinds of things you can find in the toolkit and some ways you might use them. Many of the activities come in six different background colors—blue, brown, green, orange, teal, and purple—to allow you to match up color schemes if you like.

When choosing which activities and tools to use from the Lesson Activity Toolkit, consider whether the activity or tool is intended for whole-group, small-group, pair, or individual practice. Many of the activities work well for whole-group instruction or practice, but others are better suited to small groups, pairs, or individuals. As much as possible, choose activities for whole-group instruction that allow all students to participate in some way, rather than having the class watch one student interact.

General Tips for Using Tools from the Lesson Activity Toolkit

Many of the tools in the Lesson Activity Toolkit include a ? icon. Clicking on the ? icon and reading the information will clear up most, if not all, questions you have about using the activity. You may also find that consulting the Examples file of the Lesson Activity Toolkit is useful as it includes sample activities that have been created using the different interactive activities and tools from the Lesson Activity Toolkit. The following are some general tips for using the interactive tools:

◆ The double-arrow that appears in the upper right-hand corner of some of the tools indicates that you can edit the tool (Figure 5.4). Click on the double-arrow once and the Edit mode will open. Some tools allow you to change font size, style, and color. Some also allow you to change the color of the tool itself. Other tools are intended for you to edit and input an image or text. When adding images to the tools, make sure that the image inserts into the tool. You can tell that it is inserting as you drag it over the place on the tool to add it by the plus (+) icon that appears just below your mouse arrow. For some tools the background color of the tool itself temporarily changes color as the image is inserted. Read the different options available for each tool. You will find similarities between many of them once you begin working with them. To exit the edit mode, click the double-arrow again. Now the tool is ready to use.

Figure 5.4. Using Interactive Tools

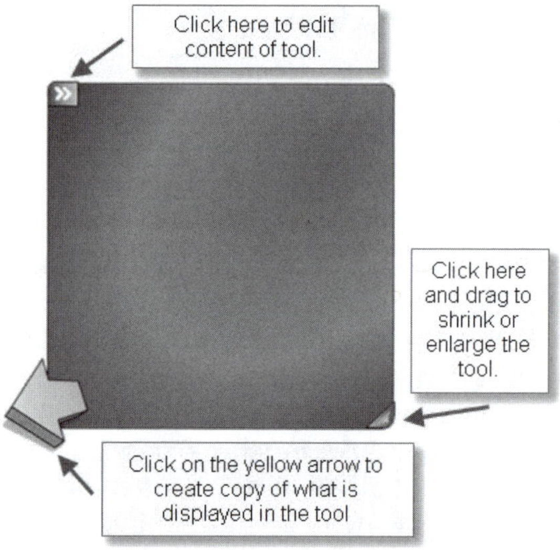

Click here to edit content of tool.

Click here and drag to shrink or enlarge the tool.

Click on the yellow arrow to create copy of what is displayed in the tool

◆ Some tools, primarily the Dice and the Hide and Reveal tools, can be enlarged or shrunk. In the lower right-hand corner you will see a triangle-shaped light blue tab that has lines on it. Clicking on it and dragging it toward the lower right-hand corner of the workspace enlarges the tool. Clicking on the tab and dragging the tool toward the upper left-hand corner shrinks the tool.

◆ Right-clicking on Dice and Hide and Reveal tools reveals a menu of options similar to those available for regular objects. You can Clone, Cut, Copy, Paste, Delete, Lock, and Order these tools.

- Other tools from the toolkit may have an Edit button in the upper left-hand corner. To edit them, click the button and the Edit mode will open. Add any text or images and make the selections requested based on the type of activity it is. When you have completed the activity, select OK and the tool will return to practice mode and be ready to use. These tools will often offer you the option to reset the activity, check the answers, and solve the activity. Some activities are immediately self-checking. Tools that say they are image tools will accept any object, including photo images, clip art, and text. However, for text you are generally better off using the tool that is designed specifically for text as it will display better. If you have grouped more than one image together or used a Pen tool to draw over something on the image to disguise it, it may not display as well in an interactive tool.

- For any of the tools in the Lesson Activity Toolkit that have a yellow arrow in a corner, clicking on the arrow will produce a copy of the text or image from the tool and place it on your page.

- Be aware that the tools and activities in the Lesson Activity Toolkit that are Flash files are space intensive. If you create a file that has many Flash files, it will generally be quite large. Images and videos can also contribute to large file sizes. Some people will find that having too many Flash files in one Notebook file can create issues for them because the file size becomes too large. Also, larger files can take longer to open.

Review of Activities and Tools from the Lesson Activity Toolkit and Ideas for Use

Note: You will find the tools listed in the chart below in the Lesson Activity Toolkit, which is found by looking in the Gallery. Be aware that when you search for the tools below, each one from tool 2 through 20 is available with blue, brown, green, orange, purple, and teal background themes. When you search for them, they are first categorized by their color and then the name of the tool. For example: Blue – Anagram, Blue – Category Sort, Blue – Hot Spots.

Tool and Description	Ideas for Use
1. Balloon Pop Pop the balloon to reveal the answer behind it.	◆ Practice any topic that has an answer.

Tool and Description	Ideas for Use
2. Anagram Unscramble the word(s).	◆ Practice spelling and word recognition.
3. Category Sort Sort words or terms into 1 to 3 categories.	◆ Sort numbers by your choice of classification. ◆ Categorize parts of the circulatory system vs. the respiratory system. ◆ Categorize nouns, verbs, and adjectives.
4. Category Sort: Image Sort images into 1 to 3 categories.	◆ Categorize images into their correct food group. ◆ Sort pictures that represent 2 different cultures into the right category.
5. Hot Spots Identify the correct spot. Built-in templates include a world map, human body, grid for graphing, Venn diagram, and a customize option.	◆ Identify the location of the vocabulary terms you choose. ◆ *Note:* If you use the customize option, insert the object you want students to identify things on first, send it to the back, and then add the identification labels.
6. Image Arrange Put the images in the correct sequence.	◆ Put images of the development of a caterpillar in order. ◆ Order images of historical events. ◆ Put pictures of a morning routine in order.
7. Image Match Match 1 to 5 images to their description.	◆ Match the image to the word it represents. ◆ Match the image to a short definition of it. ◆ Match the image to a short question or statement about it.
8. Image Select Match 1 to 18 images with their corresponding text. The images flash on the board until you touch the image. Students have 3 choices of text to match to the image.	◆ Match the image to the word represents. ◆ Match the image to its definition. ◆ Match the image to a question or statement about it.

Tool and Description	Ideas for Use
9. Keyword Match Match a word to its description.	♦ Match a term to its definition. ♦ Practice math facts. ♦ Match a question to its answer. ♦ Match a country to its capital, currency, president, etc.
10. Multiple Choice Choose the correct answer from among the 4 provided options.	♦ Choose the correct term from a description. ♦ Choose the correct description of a term. ♦ Choose the correct answer to a question or the question for the answer provided.
11. Note Reveal Present succinct notes to students. Each note is hidden until revealed.	♦ Present or review characteristics of parts of speech. ♦ Explain a sequence of steps in a process. ♦ Identify and describe characteristics of different types of clouds.
12. Pairs Create a concentration game with up to 12 pairs with both images and text.	♦ Match an image to its definition. ♦ Match a definition to its word. ♦ Match a word to its picture. ♦ Match a flag to its country. ♦ Match a continent to its outline.
13. Pull Tab Hide information off-screen using the pull tab. Type the text that you want to appear as information or directions in the text box. Also determine the tab location and label by editing it. Finally, place the tab so the text hides off-screen. Click on the pin to set the location. Pull the tab on-screen to view the instructions. Click on the blue arrow to automatically return the tab to its original location.	♦ Use for instructions for students or for yourself that you do not want to have clutter the page. ♦ Use as a way to reveal answers to questions. You can also put images in the pull tab. ♦ Use as additional information about the activity.

Tool and Description	Ideas for Use
14. Sentence Arrange Put 1 to 8 sentences in sequential order.	◆ Order the steps to put together a motor. ◆ Sequence ordinal numbers. ◆ Put the process for solving equations in order. ◆ Put the directions for making a cake in the correct sequence.
15. Tiles Hide text, images, or 1 image behind the tiles. Follow the instructions provided by clicking on the ? icon.	◆ Hide 1 image behind all of the tiles of something that is culturally relevant to what you are studying. Randomly uncover parts of the image until students guess what it is. This can be done as an introduction to a new unit and lead into a discussion to see what students know or as an activity during the unit. ◆ Put a math question on the visible side of each tile. Ask students to answer it and then they can click on each tile to reveal the correct response. ◆ Create a short *Jeopardy* game with the tiles by putting numbers for point values on the visible tile. Click on the tile to reveal the question and then the teacher can confirm the correct answer or click on the tile after the question provided by the teacher has been answered to show the correct answer.
16. Timeline Reveal Put up to 10 dates on the timeline with a description of their significance.	◆ Have students create a timeline for their own lives with significant events for them to share with you or the class as a get-to-know-you activity or as practice with creating a timeline. ◆ Create a timeline of your life to share with students so they can get to know you. ◆ Create a historical timeline for events you are studying. ◆ Create a unit timeline to preview what you will be studying and when.

Tool and Description	Ideas for Use
17. Vortex Sort terms into their category by placing them in the correct vortex. Up to 16 terms can be used. If the term is improperly categorized, it will be rejected from the vortex.	♦ Categorize eating customs of 2 different countries. ♦ Sort numbers by even and odd. ♦ Identify whether equations are balanced or unbalanced. ♦ Categorize the beliefs of Piaget vs. Freud. ♦ Categorize traits of 2 characters in a book.
18. Vortex: Image Sort images into their category by placing them in the correct vortex. Up to 16 images can be used. If the image is improperly categorized, it will be rejected from the vortex.	♦ Categorize farm vs. zoo animals. ♦ Categorize images that represent cultural elements of 2 different countries. ♦ Categorize amphibians and reptiles. ♦ Categorize nouns and verbs with pictorial representations of them.
19. Word Biz Answer 1 to 8 questions by spelling out the answer.	♦ Conjugate a verb. ♦ Answer questions about a culture of study.
20. Word Guess Guess the word in a format similar to *Hangman*. Choose from 1 of 3 modes to earn points: basketball, soccer, and the tomato splat. Clues can be provided.	♦ Practice challenging spelling words. ♦ Use the clues and have students answer questions.
21. Checker Tool The checker tool allows you to input an answer and check whether it is correct.	♦ Use for activities where students use the interactive whiteboard as a station. Students can choose from various options and drag their choice into the checker tool to self-check.
22. Click and Reveal: Circle, Rectangle, Star, Square, Triangle Click once on the shape to reveal the answer that you hide below.	♦ Use this as another variation on how to reveal questions or answers.

Tool and Description	Ideas for Use
23. Color Chooser Click on the square to show a different color. Selecting the Edit icon allows you to choose how many colors you would like to be used.	◆ Use for colors practice in world-language classrooms. ◆ Use for counting and categorizing in elementary classrooms. Clicking the yellow arrow produces a shape you can manipulate on the workspace. ◆ Use as a selection tool for groups if each group is assigned a color.
24. Crossword Create a crossword with 1 to 10 clues. Type in clues and answers or drag them in from other sources.	◆ Use for an activity on individual computers or as station activity to practice vocabulary. Writing more rigorous clues will make the activity more challenging.
25. Dice: Black, Red, Blue, Green, Pink This tool is an interactive die. It comes in the colors identified above. There are also dice that say the number you roll in English, French, and Spanish.	◆ Use for practice with probability. ◆ Use as dice for a game. There are many different sports fields in the Gallery that can be used to make steps toward scoring home runs or making goals in a game. Roll the die for a turn and use in conjunction with the scoreboard.
26. Dice: Image Roll images rather than numbers. Edit the die and add 6 images. This die is limited to 6 images, whereas the Random Image tool is very similar and allows many more images.	◆ Use for vocabulary practice. Ask students to identify or describe the image, ask them questions about the image, have them ask you questions about the image. Practice can be done in written or oral form.
27. Dice: Keyword Roll words rather than numbers. Edit the die and type in 6 words. Try the Random Text tool if you would like to use more than 6 terms and would like to use more words as part of the text.	◆ Use as preview/preassessment of new terms. Ask students to write as much as they can about the word that is rolled. ◆ Have students work in pairs to explain the term orally or in writing. ◆ Use a timer tool and ask students to write as many unique sentences or questions with the term in them as possible.

Tool and Description	Ideas for Use
28. Dice: Numbers Roll a die that has numbers rather than dots.	♦ Use more than 1 die for addition, subtraction, multiplication, or division problems. ♦ Use to practice saying numbers out loud. Line up as many dice as you want in a row to create larger numbers. ♦ Roll at the end of the hour to see if students need to do even or odd homework problems.
29. Domino Generator: Black or Yellow Click on the domino once to create a pattern. Then click on the gray arrow to reproduce it. Continue until you have as many dominos as you would like.	♦ Generate dominoes to practice addition, subtraction, and multiplication. Students can add the top and bottom numbers together, subtract the bottom from the top or multiply the two together.
30. Domino Generator: Image This domino allows you to add text or an image to each half of the domino.	♦ Use for students to practice matching images to their word. ♦ Create a set of dominoes that has synonyms and antonyms and have them play the game as a station activity. ♦ Have students make their own set of dominoes for new words they are learning or for something like the synonyms and antonyms for another student to play.
31. Firecracker This tool counts down from 10 to 1 and makes the sound of an explosion when it is done. Click on the end of the wick to activate it.	♦ Use this tool as a way to get students seated or ready to begin. Let them know that when they hear the noise they need to be ready to start class or the next activity.
32. Note Reveal: Left or Right Click on the ? to reveal a text box in which you can write a brief direction or explanation. You must choose whether the note will open to the left or right.	♦ Use this tool to reveal short instructions or a brief explanation of something for students or other teachers.

Tool and Description	Ideas for Use
33. Question Flipper 1 This square-shaped tool allows you to put text on both sides of the square. Click on the double-arrow in the upper-left hand corner to edit the text and follow the instructions. You can edit the text style, color, and size, as well as the color of the Flipper tool. Once you customize the Flipper the way you would like it, use the Clone option by right-clicking on the Flipper to create the exact same settings as were used for the original Flipper.	♦ Use this tool for a simple matching game by leaving one side blank and typing text on the other. Create the match on one of the other squares and click on all of the Flipper tools so they face down. ♦ Use the tool to practice questions and answers, definitions, and vocabulary words, synonyms, and antonyms. ♦ For world-language instruction, put a word in the second language on one side and a description of the word on the other side in the same language. Students should guess what the word is from its description.
34. Question Flipper 2 This long, rectangular question Flipper works the same way that Question Flipper 1 does. See explanation above.	♦ Provide an answer to a question and have students generate the question. ♦ Create a fill-in-the-blank question for students to solve for the missing word or number.
35. Question Flipper: Image This square question Flipper tool works the same way as Question Flipper 1, with the exception that it allows both images and text to be used. An image can be placed on one side with text on the other. Two images can also be used. To add the image, first click on the double-arrow in the upper left-hand corner. Make sure that Image is selected at the bottom of the Edit options. Then, drag and drop the image in the space that says "Drag image here."	♦ Put an image on each side of the Flipper tool. Ask students to determine how they are related orally or in writing. ♦ Put an image on each side and ask students to write a sentence that includes the two words. ♦ Put a question word on the text side and an image on the other. Ask students to form a question about the image with the included question word. ♦ Put an image on one side and a word or definition on the other. Ask students to determine if the image and the word or definition are a match.

Tool and Description	Ideas for Use
36. Question Tool Type an answer in the tool. Click on it to reveal the answer. See examples in the Lesson Activity Toolkit.	♦ Use this tool with a diagram. Use an arrow to point to various things in the diagram and use the Question tool as a way to click and identify what the item is. ♦ Use with a diagram where one item needs to be identified. Use more than one Question tool to provide answer options. In the Edit menu, identify the correct answer with the tick (green check mark) and the incorrect ones with a cross (red X).
37. Random Card Generator This tool randomly generates playing cards.	♦ Use for a probability activity. ♦ Use the face values of the cards for mathematical calculations like addition, subtraction, and division. ♦ Use as part of a card game.
38. Random Consonant Generator This tool randomly generates consonants.	♦ Use for a word game. How many adjectives can you think of that start with the generated letter? ♦ Write a sentence that only uses the letter generated for the first letter of each word in the sentence.
39. Random Group Generator This tool will randomly select students to form 2 to 18 groups. Type in the names of up to 36 students and select the number of groups you would like formed.	♦ Use it to create new pairs for students to work with once a week or more often. ♦ Use it to create groups for projects and discussions.
40. Random Image Chooser This tool will randomly select 1 to 36 different images. Select the number of images you would like to use and drag an image into as many blank squares in the tool as you would like.	♦ Use as a vocabulary practice activity: identify the picture, define what it is, write a sentence or question about it, etc. ♦ Use as a review game, giving students points as individuals or teams for being able to do one of the things from either of the previous ideas. ♦ Select 2 or more of the pictures and ask students to identify a relationship between the 2 or compare and contrast them.

Tool and Description	Ideas for Use
41. Random Image Tool This Dice tool allows you add numerous images to it.	◆ Use it to practice vocabulary by identifying the word from the image, writing a sentence or question about the word, writing a definition of the word and more. ◆ Turn the previous activity into a game. Award points to groups or teams for the best descriptions, questions, definitions, etc. Combine with the Scoreboard tool to keep points. Use extra scorekeeper tools if you need to for additional teams.
42. Random Letter Generator This tool randomly generates consonants. Use the yellow arrow to inject the letter onto the page.	◆ Generate and inject 4 or more letters, making sure at least one is a vowel. Ask students to create as many words with that set of letters as possible. ◆ Generate and inject 4 or more letters. Ask students to create a sentence where a word in the sentence starts with each of the different letters. As a variation, ask students to also illustrate the sentence.
43. Random Number Generator This tool randomly generates numbers. You can set the range of numbers it will produce.	◆ Tell the square root of the number generated, what plus what equals the number, create a subtraction problem that equals the generated number, etc. ◆ Guess the next number that will be generated. This is a fun activity for world-language classes.
44. Random Text Tool This Dice tool allows you to add many text selections to it.	◆ Practice math facts. ◆ Write or say a definition for the term. ◆ State the term that is being described. ◆ Inject a few of the terms from the dice and ask students to come up with a sentence that uses all of them, a connection between the words, etc.

Tool and Description	Ideas for Use
45. Random Vowel Generator This tool randomly selects vowels.	◆ Write a word that uses the vowel as a long vowel. ◆ Write a word that uses the same vowel twice in the word. ◆ Tell your partner the first word you can think of that has that vowel in it. ◆ Write the longest word you can that has that vowel in it.
46. Random Word Chooser This tool allows you to input up to 36 names or words. It will then randomly select one of those names or words.	◆ Use as a way to pick students to participate in class activities. ◆ Use for a word game. Students need to write a question, definition, sentence, draw a picture, etc. of the word that is picked.
47. Scoreboard This tool allows you to keep track of scores for team games, both adding and subtracting points.	◆ Use this in conjunction with any game for which you want to keep a score for 2 teams.
48. Sudoku This tool generates Sudoku boards.	◆ Use as an activity for students to do on individual computers or using the interactive whiteboard as a station. ◆ Generate a game and print it for students to do at their desk if they finish work early and/or allow a couple students to do it at the board. Print the solution or don't close the game in the Notebook file to make sure you don't lose the solution.

Tool and Description	Ideas for Use
49. Spinner This tool will spin and land on a color. There may be up to 12 colors that you can choose. Each section of the spinner also allows text.	♦ Use the spinner to play games. The color or word the spinner lands on can correspond to a type of question students need to answer. The spinner can also be paired with a game board and be used to determine to what color spot on the board you can move. At that spot students can answer a question. ♦ Use the spinner for verb conjugation practice for world-language classes. Put the subject pronouns in as the text, one per slice of the spinner. Give students different verbs to conjugate on their dry erase board to hold up for you to check. ♦ Use the spinner for vocabulary practice. In each spinner section put things like a sentence, picture, definition, question, antonym, synonym, etc. Provide students with a word. Each time they spin they must provide what is on the spinner section for the word identified by the teacher. You can also use a second spinner or the Random Text Tool as another way to generate the words.
50. Text Splitter This tool will split the text you put in the box. If you put in a word, it will split it into its individual letters and inject them onto your workspace. If you put in a sentence, it will split the sentence into its individual words.	♦ See how many words you can make with the letters in the split words. ♦ Enlarge the text that comes out and use for a word or sentence unscramble activity. ♦ Unscramble the sentence and then add at least 2 adjectives and a connecting word to it to make it more interesting and complex.
51. Vote Tool This tool will keep track of votes on one topic.	♦ Take hot lunch count. ♦ Use 2 Vote tools and label each with a topic. Students can vote for their preference. Results can be used for a class discussion or debate when students have to provide a reason for why they voted the way they did.

Tool and Description	Ideas for Use
52. Word Generator This tool will allow you to input up to 15 words. You can also put in numbers and other characters. They can be generated in order or randomly.	♦ Ask students to make associations between the 2 or more words that are generated. ♦ Write the shortest or longest sentence you can with the generated words. ♦ Define the generated word or use it in a sentence that shows its meaning. ♦ Solve the math problem that is generated.

Graphics Tools from the Lesson Activity Toolkit

The Graphics folder in the Lesson Activity Toolkit folder offers other valuable resources for designing your lessons. The resources in this folder are created with the same color scheme as some of the interactive tools to allow you to create lessons with a professional, finished look. The following chart provides an overview of the resources you can find and some ideas on how you might use them.

Lesson Activity Toolkit Graphics	Uses
1. Bars and Boxes Includes options for a title bar, square and rectangle in blue, brown, green, orange, purple, and teal.	♦ Use as a way to make text for instructions or other lesson information stand out from the page.
2. Borders Includes activity and page borders that are outlined in blue, brown, green, orange, purple, and teal.	♦ Use as a background layer to make activities stand out from the page and look more polished. ♦ See examples of how they are used in the *Examples* folder of the *Lesson Activity Toolkit*.
3. Icons Icons are color-coded in the 6 colors to blend with your lesson. Icons include back buttons, pointers, question marks, exclamation points, check marks, and other shadowed symbols.	♦ Use icons to draw students' attention to a particular lesson feature or to give them directions for a next step in the lesson.

Lesson Activity Toolkit Graphics	Uses
4. Labels and Buttons Two versions of buttons are included in the 6 main lesson colors, a circle and a rectangle. There is 1 editable rectangle label per color scheme. Double-clicking on the label opens a text box and allows you to edit it.	♦ Use the buttons to link to a website, audio, video, or document file, or to another page. Group text over the button to identify an instruction. ♦ Use the label to identify items on your page.
5. Pull Tabs Hide information off-screen using the pull tab. Type the text that you want to appear as information or directions in the text box. Also determine the tab location and label by editing it. Finally, place the tab so the text hides off-screen. Click on the pin to set the location. Pull the tab on-screen to view the instructions. Click on the blue arrow to automatically return the tab to its original location.	♦ Use to hide lesson instructions or questions off-screen to avoid cluttering the page with too much information.

To see examples of how the graphics have been used on sample lesson pages, see the Examples file of the Lesson Activity Toolkit. There are many sample ideas in this section, divided by category. You will also find examples of lessons from different content areas at the SMART Exchange: http://exchange.smarttech.com/.

Other Interactive Lesson Tools from the Gallery Essentials

Some other useful interactive tools are found in the Interactive and Multimedia section of the Gallery Essentials folder, also found in the Gallery. Some are subject specific, but others can be used for a variety of subjects. Search the subject files listed, browse the Interactive and Multimedia subsection, or do a general search of the Gallery by the name listed in the chart. The chart below will give you a general description of the tool and some basic ideas for its use. Most of the tools just need to be dragged onto the workspace and they are ready to use.

Tool and Description	Ideas for Use
1. Calculator This tool works as a regular basic calculator does. Use the yellow arrow to inject the calculation onto the workspace.	♦ Use for any basic calculations.
2. Calendar: Weekly Select Edit to choose the month and year. Then click on Generate Calendar. Enlarge by clicking and dragging the lower right-hand corner of the object. Use the yellow arrow to inject a calendar onto the workspace.	♦ Use the calendar to have a visual aid for discussing upcoming events or to discuss project timelines with students. ♦ Use a shape tool or highlighter to identify important dates. ♦ Use the injected version of the calendar to write in text for tests and homework assignments.
3. Clock: Analog (Current Time)	♦ Enlarge it on the page and use it as tool to explain how clocks work. ♦ Practice the current time. ♦ Use as a visual reminder of the time to transition between activities.
4. Clock	♦ Great for teaching time in any language. Combine with a dry erase board for an activity where all students can participate. A student at the board can change the times on the clock and write an answer on the board with which students can check their answers.
5. Timer and Timer 2	♦ Use as a countdown for any timed activity or to just to keep an activity moving so students have a defined period of time in which to complete it. ♦ Also use to count up to a predetermined amount of minutes.

Tool and Description	Ideas for Use
6. Hundreds Chart Touch a number on the chart with the colored pen of your choice and when the number flips it will show in that color.	♦ Use to practice numbers in any language. ♦ Use as a visual for counting even and odd numbers, by fives, tens, etc. ♦ Ask students to say or write down the number that you or another student touches.
7. Dice-Consonants or Dice-Vowels Roll the die to generate a consonant or vowel, depending upon the die you chose.	♦ Write a word that has the consonant you roll somewhere in it. ♦ Using more than 1 die, have students generate as many words as possible with the combination rolled. ♦ See ideas from dice in the prior chart.
8. Flip a Coin Click Start to begin flipping the coin and Stop to discontinue the flipping.	♦ Use to make a decision as you would by flipping a regular coin. ♦ Use for math applications.
9. Compass* The top yellow handle of the compass will rotate the compass. The other two yellow handles on the left will drag the compass to a new location on the workspace. The yellow handle on the right will open the compass to set the angle. Change the pen color by clicking on the pen and then selecting the Pen icon in the main toolbar. Select the color you would like and the pen color will change. To create a circle, click on the pen in the compass and draw the circle.	♦ Demonstrate circumference and bisecting lines. Combine with the interactive ruler to find the radius and take other measurements.
10. Multiple Dice Create up to 8 dice that will roll simultaneously. Click on the yellow arrow to inject the numerical forms of what was rolled onto your page to practice addition. You also have the option to edit the dice color.	♦ Use to practice addition and multiplication. ♦ Practice probability.

Tool and Description	Ideas for Use
11. Protractor* Move the protractor to the desired location of the angle by dragging it on the board and measure.	♦ Use the line tools to create different angles to demonstrate how to use a protractor. ♦ Set up a practice activity in the Notebook software that students can do at the board as a station activity with click and reveal or checker tool so they can self-check their work.
12. Protractor: 360 degrees* Click on the white handle with the green outline and drag the protractor to the desired angle. Click on the green arrow to inject the angle onto the workspace. Angles will automatically have the degrees listed. To remove the answer, right click on the angle and select Group and then Ungroup. Delete the number and then regroup the rest of the angle. Alternatively, use the magic eraser effect to hide the angle degrees. Use the eraser to reveal the answers when students are ready with answers.	♦ Use this protractor to create sample angles to explain to students. ♦ Use this protractor to create the angles you will have students measure with this or the 180-degree protractor.
13. Interactive Ruler* Set to metric or Imperial. Move the arrows on one or both ends so they line up with the ends of the object you are measuring. Click on the gray arrow and the length will be calculated by the ruler as well.	♦ Use to demonstrate how to use a ruler. ♦ Set up measuring practice activities that allow students to use the Interactive Ruler. Ask students to first record their measurement and then allow them to check their answer with the automeasurement.
14. Fraction Maker Create fractions by writing in the numerator and denominator. Click the gray arrow to create the fraction.	♦ Have students create different fractions with the tool and then simplify them. Use two different colored pens to highlight the difference between the numerator and the denominator.

Tool and Description	Ideas for Use
15. Flash Cards Create basic addition, subtraction, multiplication, and division flash-cards. Choose the level of difficulty, type, and number of cards.	◆ Use for whole-group or small-group station review of basic math facts.
16. Slope of a Line Calculate the line slope.	◆ Calculate the slope of the line and then check your work with the interactive tool.
17. Thermometer Practice the temperature in Fahrenheit and Celsius. Show or hide the electronic reading.	◆ Use for practice of reading a thermometer. Ask students to take different readings as a station activity. They can check their work by revealing the digital reading. ◆ Ask students to convert Fahrenheit to Celsius. They can check their work by changing from having the thermometer read in Fahrenheit to Celsius and by looking at the digital reading.
18. Periodic Table Click on the element to display its properties. Click on Instructions in the activity for further information.	◆ Introduce and explain the Periodic Table. ◆ Practice the elements with the game feature as a station activity or on an individual computer.
19. Drums, Saxophone, etc. Instrument images with audio for what it sounds like. Click on the speaker icon in the corner of the instrument. Look up instruments by their name.	◆ Introduce students to the sounds different instruments make with the visual aid of what the instrument looks like. ◆ Discuss the different features of the instruments.
20. Pitch Explorer Click on the xylophone to hear difference pitches.	◆ Use as a station activity to listen to and practice pitches. ◆ Record and play back a sound pattern with the recording feature.

*Measurement tools in the table above with an asterisk by them can also be accessed in the main toolbar in Notebook 10.6. Look for the icon that has a protractor and a compass in it. If you hover over the icon it will be identified as Measurement Tools. Clicking on the icon will give you a horizontal drop-down menu that provides you the option to insert a ruler, protractor, Goedreieck protractor, or a compass onto your workspace.

Additional Interactive Resources

Audiovisual Resources

Some other resources that may be of interest to you are images and text that have audio already embedded. By perusing the Interactive and Multimedia section of the Gallery Essentials folder, you will find the numbers one through twenty, the alphabet, instruments, and a selection of other words with embedded audio with which students can interact. Click and drag or double-click on anything that you would like to use to add it to your page.

Also in the Interactive and Multimedia section you will find a selection of interactive tools that explain or demonstrate a process. The majority of the content is focused on science, math and language skills.

Navigation Buttons

Some other tools of use found in the Gallery Essentials folder are Navigation Buttons (Figure 5.5, page 120). These buttons are filed in the Administration and Evaluation folder. Use these buttons to navigate your lesson if students need to move from one page to another based on the information on the page. You can create your own buttons as well by using a shape or image related to the topic of your lesson. The difference in using these Flash-based navigation buttons is that they give the sense of movement when pressed. To link to another page, rather than to a website, right-click on the object that you want to use to redirect the student to another page. Choose Link from the drop-down menu. From your options in the window that pops up, choose to Link to a Page in this File and then select the page to which you would like to link. To finish, choose the option to launch by clicking the object and then select OK. There are various games that have been created using the link to another page feature. One such game has lots of circles of different colors, each of which has been linked to another page in the Notebook file with a question on the page to answer. Students can throw a koosh ball at the board to activate the circle which will lead to the question to answer or can touch it with their finger. You can search for the koosh ball game template with your favorite Internet search engine or you can also find it, along with other game templates at: http://smartboardtips.wikispaces.com/Games+Templates.

Figure 5.5. Navigation Buttons

Sample Navigation Buttons

Organizing and Synthesizing Information

Tables

Tables can serve many instructional purposes and are a great way to organize and synthesize information. Here are a few ways you might use a table on the interactive whiteboard:

♦ Present new information to students about which they can answer questions or discuss.

♦ Allow students to categorize text and/or objects as a prelesson activity or after they have worked with the lesson material.

♦ Create a review game like *Jeopardy* using the cell shades to cover up the questions or answers.

♦ Create a memory or concentration game using objects and/or text along with the cell shades.

♦ Ask students to create their own table to synthesize information.

Considerations When Creating Tables

Tables are useful tools for organizing information for nearly any subject matter. You can create your own tables in Notebook using the line or shape tools or you can use the Table feature of Notebook. Before you begin to create your table, have an idea of the type of content you would like to use and how you plan to organize it. Are you planning to put only text in the table or will you also use other objects? Will you need to color code some of the cells in a different color to highlight particular information? What text style and size will you use? How many cells will you likely need?

Table Creation

To create a table, click on the Table icon in the main toolbar. Once you do so, a grid will appear that allows you to select the table size. You can select a size of up to eight rows by eight columns (Figure 5.6). Another way to add a table is by going to the Insert menu and selecting Table from the drop-down menu.

Figure 5.6. Tables

split cells			hide cells with cell shades	fill with text	
adjust column width and row height			infinitely clone	delete cells	change cell color

When your table is first inserted, you will see the dashed blue line around the edge of the table, a square handle in the upper left-hand corner, the triangle-shaped down arrow in the upper right-hand corner, and the gray circular handle in the lower right-hand corner. The square handle allows you to move the table location, the circular handle lets you minimize and maximize the table size, and the down arrow gives you access to the drop-down menu with table editing options. To begin working with the table, make any sizing adjustments to it and then move the table to where you would like to be on the page. You can always adjust the location again later. The following whole table editing options are available to you in the drop-down menu:

- ♦ Clone
- ♦ Cut
- ♦ Copy
- ♦ Paste
- ♦ Delete
- ♦ Locking
- ♦ Flip
- ♦ Order
- ♦ Infinite Cloner
- ♦ Link
- ♦ Sound

- Add Table Shade
- Remove Table Shade
- Adjust Size
- Properties

You have worked with most of the editing options in previous chapters of the book so the focus here is on the ones that are available only when working with tables.

Add a Table Shade

This feature allows you to add a shade to each cell that will cover the information underneath. This is useful if you want to expose the information one cell at a time so students have to figure out what is underneath the cells. It can also be used for a basic type of concentration or memory game. To cover the cells again, use the Undo button in the main toolbar. The table shade is likely the last thing you would add upon completing the table, as you will want to have all of the information in the cells before covering them. If you decide that you do not want to have a table shade on the table after all, you will need to select Remove Table Shade from the drop-down menu.

Adjust Size

If you would like to autoadjust the size of the table cells so they are uniform, select Adjust Size from the drop-down menu. You will be given the following options: Make Same Height, Make Same Width, and Make Same Size. If you want all cells to be the same size, use Make Same Size. Otherwise, select the option that you would like to adjust the cells.

Properties

If you would like to adjust the line size or style of the table or change the fill to a color, select Properties. When you select a line size or style, it will apply your choice to the entire table. The same will happen for the fill effects. If you would like to make certain cells, rows, columns, or sections of the table stand out, you can select that part of the table and apply the effect you would like to it. To select one cell, click on it with the mouse and you will see that cell darken. To select any other segment of the table, click on the cell you would like to start with and then drag the mouse across the rest of the cells you want to change. When you stop moving the mouse, you will see a transparent green rectangle appear on top of the cells you selected. You can now make the line or fill adjustments you would like and they will apply to the selected cells. Remember that if you make the cells somewhat transparent and you have a color applied to the page background, those two colors will mix. You can always place a white rectangle behind the table to avoid the color mixing if that is a concern.

Inactive Table

If you click off the table and need to make the table active again so you can access the drop-down menu or any of the table handles, you will need to perform a marquis select on the table (Figure 5.7). To do a marquis select, click on the page at a corner outside of the table and drag the mouse over the top of it until you see the handles and drop-down menu arrow appear again.

Figure 5.7. Active Table

| split cells | | | hide cells with cell shades | fill with text | | The table is active when the dashed blue line and handles appear around the edge of it. |
| adjust column width and row height | | | infinitely clone | delete cells | change cell color | |

Adding Rows and Columns

If you find that you do not have enough rows or columns, you can add them. However, do consider that adding more columns or rows than the eight in the default may result in your needing to use a very small text size in the table cells. To add an additional column, click and drag over the cells in the column that are to the left of the new column you will want to add. Once you see the transparent green rectangle appear over the cells in the column, right-click. Upon right-clicking you will see the following options:

- ◆ Merge Cells: This merges any cells that are highlighted together.

- ◆ Insert Column: This inserts a column to the right of the highlighted column.

- ◆ Delete Column: This deletes the entire highlighted column.

- ◆ Delete Cells: This deletes any cells that are highlighted.

- ◆ Add Cell Shade: This adds the cell shades to the individual cells that are highlighted.

- ◆ Properties: This takes you to the Properties area and lets you change the lines or fill of the cells in the highlighted area.

Selecting a row rather than a column will give you the same options, except that rows will be added automatically below the highlighted column.

Enlarging Rows and Columns

If you want to adjust the size of columns or rows in your table so they are not uniform in size, hover the mouse over the line that you would like to move. When you see a line with arrows at each end, click on the line and start moving the mouse in the direction you would like to move the row or column. When you start moving the mouse you will see a thick red line appear that represents the new location for the row or column line. When you stop moving the mouse and remove your finger from the mouse, the line will move to the new location. This will work with all lines, except the top line of the table. If you perform the same action on the top line of the table, the entire table will either move up or down, depending upon the direction in which you move the line.

Editing Individual Cells

You can also edit individual cells. Right-clicking on one cell gives you these options:

- Split: Choose Split to have the option to split the cells in six different ways.
- Delete Cells: This deletes the selected cell.
- Add Cell Shade: This adds the cell shade to the selected cell.
- Properties: This takes you to the Properties area and lets you change the lines or fill of the cell.

Adding Text

You can add text to a table. To add text, start by typing the text in a text box outside the table. If you want to change the color or style, do that as well. You may also want to consider centering the text in the text box, depending upon how you want the text to appear in the table. Experiment a bit with how you like the text to align in the cell. Once you have the text you would like for the table, drag it into the cell where it belongs. You will see a blue outline appear around the inside of the cell before the text is added. If you want to remove the text from the cell, click on it and drag it out. Another option is to create the new text you want to appear in the cell and just drag it in on top of the old text and it will cover up the previous text.

Adding Objects

You can also add objects to the table. You may want objects for a simple memory game or you can also use them to have students categorize the object into a correct category. If you are going to have students categorize, you might create the category header with a picture and have students put in text below it, or vice versa. Either way, for this type of activity you will want to leave the objects or text that are not part of the header outside of the table so students can add them in to the correct category. Objects will drag into the table the same way that text does. You can set the objects or text outside of the table to be infinite cloners if they will be used in more than one category or if you just want to be able to see the object choices represented outside of the table.

Centering Objects

On occasion when you add objects to the table they may appear off center. A way to adjust for that is by using the Shape tool to create a square. You will want the line and fill color of the square to be the same color as the table cell color into which you will be inserting the square. The way to keep it simple is to keep the cell colors white and to make an entirely white square. Insert the object you want to be centered in the cell onto your workspace. Move that object so it is centered over your white square and then group the two objects together. Now when you drag the object into the table it should look more centered. If you are going to create multiple objects this way, it will save time to make the square you create an infinite cloner so you can drag a new square off the infinite cloner, add and center your object, group the two together and then add the new object to the table.

Adding Text and Objects to the Same Cell

You can also add a word and object to the same cell, but that requires that they first be grouped together. If you first add an object to a cell and then try to add some text to accompany the object, the text will cover the object. To avoid this problem, group the text and the object together the way you would like them to appear in the cell. Once they are grouped, they can be added to the cell and you will be able to see both of them.

Adding Tables to the Gallery

You may create and format a table that serves multiple purposes or that you simply want to use again. If you would like to reuse the table, add it to the Gallery. First, make sure your My Content folder is open (or another folder that you have created in that area). Remember that to move the table you need to do a marquis select to return it to the state of being an object. Once the table is ready to be moved, click on the square handle and drag the table to the My Content folder in the Gallery. You will notice the faded rectangle accompanied by a plus sign that appears over the table when it is ready to be added to the Gallery. Remove your finger from the mouse and drop the table into the Gallery. Make sure to label your table using something that will make it easy for you to find again in a search.

If you prefer, you can add the whole Notebook page to the Gallery. This would make sense if you want to keep the format of the page that the table is on, as well as the table itself. To add the page to the Gallery, make sure you are in the Page View mode. Then click on the down-arrow of the page you would like to add and select Add Page to Gallery from the drop-down menu that appears. Once the page is added, make sure to label it.

Making Your Own Table with the Line Tool

There may be times when you want to create your own table from scratch. To do so, you can use the Line tool and/or the Shape tool. If you use the Line tool, you may find it handy to use the duplicate feature to clone certain lines so they are the exact same length. Before you start duplicating you may want to change the line style and color. Once you have your lines situated where you would like them to be, you can group them together. Remember that if you create a table this way, the color of the page background will show through into your table. To solve that problem, create a shape with the Shape tool that matches the size of the table by drawing the shape over the lines of the edge of your table. By right-clicking on that shape, you can adjust the line and fill colors. Once you have done so, right click on your object and select Order and then Send Backward. Now, you can group the table and the other object together and the background color of the page will not impact the table. At this point you can resize the table and add any text or other objects to it.

Creating Your Own Tables with the Shape Tool

You can also create your own table with the Shape tool. One benefit of creating your own table with lines or shapes is having the ability to manipulate text or objects on top of the table without them becoming a physical part of the table. This type of table also allows more flexibility for the exact placement of the text or object in the table. I have created a table in this way when making verb conjugation charts to be able to move text around more freely and to highlight verb irregularities using a different background color from other parts of the chart. Similar to the Line tool-created chart, create the shape that is to be the basis for each cell of your chart and then duplicate it. If you intend to make any line color or style changes, do so before you duplicate the shape. You can also make color changes to the fill of the shape now before you duplicate it. Use the Alignment tool (found in the Format menu) to snap the objects into line. Place the shapes together to form the table and then make any fill changes to the individual shapes. Make any final changes to the fill or line style before you group all of the shapes together to form the table. If you plan to add any text to the table that will always appear in this particular chart, add that before grouping and then group the text and the table together. If this is the standard table you need for the activity before it is modified for more specific information, now would be a good time to add it to the My Content folder of the Gallery. Drag it in and relabel it for future use. Finish the table on your workspace by adding the rest of the necessary information.

Venn Diagrams

Using Precreated Resources

There is an assortment of ready-to-use Venn diagrams in the Gallery. To find the existing resources, search for the phrase *Venn diagram* using the Search tool in the Gallery. Your search will return a selection of Related Folders, Pictures, and Notebook Files and Pages. The information contained in the Related Folders section, will be the same as that in the Pictures and the Notebook Files and Pages. If you are looking for a premade diagram, you will want to explore the Notebook Files and Pages section and choose one that meets your needs. When you find something you like, drag it onto the page. Remember that you will not be able to manipulate the size and orientation of the circles of the Venn diagram on the Notebook Pages as they create a page background. If you would like to create your own, you can start with the Pictures section. This section has the circle outlines and shadowed inlays for the Venn diagrams. Drag as many circle outlines and inlays as you would like to use onto the page. If you do not like the colors, you can edit them as you would edit any shape. Access the object properties by right-clicking on the object. From there you can edit the transparency and change the line style and fill color. If you plan to adjust the size of the object, duplicate the size you want and then edit the properties to ensure both circles stay the same size. You also can always click and drag the object to the size you want. Once you have chosen the properties you would like and moved the object into place, group the objects together and lock them into place.

Creating a Modified Venn Diagram

With Venn diagrams, sometimes it seems that circles can limit the space that you have to write in the text when you begin comparing and contrasting information. You may want to try a square version of the Venn diagram (Figure 5.8, page 128). You can create your own by using the square Shape tool from the main toolbar. Holding down the Shift key while you drag the shape to size keeps the shape from distorting. Once you have the size you would like, duplicate the shape. From there, make any adjustments you want to the fill and lines of the object. When you are done, group and lock the objects into place; they now are ready to be labeled.

Figure 5.8. Square Venn Diagram

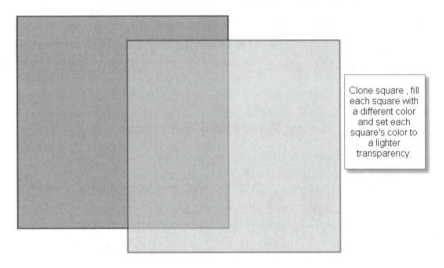

Clone square , fill each square with a different color and set each square's color to a lighter transparency.

Using the Dual Screen Feature with a Venn Diagram

There may be times when you will want to use the Dual Screen feature of Notebook along with a Venn diagram. The Dual Screen feature allows you to see two Notebook pages at the same time. By using this feature, you can have the Venn diagram on one page and the information you would like to drag onto it and classify on a second page. Clicking on text boxes or objects that are on one page lets you drag them into the Venn diagram. To activate this feature, click on the icon in the main toolbar that looks like two pages with corners bent on a blue screen background. If you hover your mouse over the top of this icon it will identify it as Single/Dual Screen Display. Clicking on this icon activates the dual screen. The page that is active when you click on the icon will always appear on the right side. To move it to the left, click once on the Next Page icon in the main toolbar represented by the blue arrow pointing right. You are now ready to move information to your Venn diagram. A limitation of the Dual Screen feature is that the text appears smaller as it has to be shrunk to show both pages together. You can adjust for this by making the text or images you classify a bit bigger. When you are ready to exit Dual Screen mode, click once on the Single/Dual Screen Display icon in the main toolbar. The icon will appear differently when you are in dual screen mode, as it will only show one page in the icon, representing the mode you will return to by clicking on the icon.

Pinning Pages

Another feature that works with the Dual Screen Display is the Pin Page tool (Figure 5.9). This tool is useful if you would like to pin the page on the left while in Dual Screen Display mode so it will not move. This feature allows you to scroll through the following pages in the Notebook document to access that information and add it to your Venn diagram without losing the Venn diagram in the scrolling. This tool is not generally part of the default settings of your main toolbar, but you can add it. Do so by right-clicking on a gray area of the main toolbar and the Customize Toolbar window will open. Look for the icon that resembles a thumb tack. Click on it and drag it to the location you would like it to be in the main toolbar. You will see a blue spacer appear in between icons to show where the new icon will be added. Choose Done in the Customize Toolbar window to exit and return to the Notebook pages. Click on the Pin Page icon once to apply it. It will automatically pin the page that is on the left side. To scroll through and view other pages, click on the Next Page icon various times and you will see that the page stays pinned and new pages are brought into view. To remove the Pin Page feature, click on the Pin Page icon in the main toolbar once.

Figure 5.9. Pinning a Page

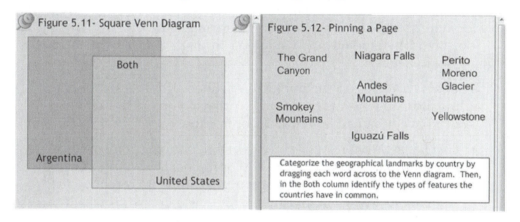

Using the Interactive Whiteboard to Assess Student Progress

Another powerful use for the interactive whiteboard is as a tool to assess student progress. There are a variety of resources in the Notebook software that aid a teacher in creating quick and useful formative assessments to check for understanding of the material students are learning. One place to look for creating such assessments is the Lesson Activity Toolkit. Some tools you may want to try out include the following activities:

♦ Category sort

♦ Image select

♦ Keyword match

- Multiple choice

- Sentence arrange

- Vortex

There are many other tools in the toolkit that may be of use for your subject area. Refer back to the charts earlier in the chapter for ideas about the above activities and the other tools.

You also can assess student progress by providing students with:

- Yes/No, True/False, Logical/Illogical, or other similar questions;

- Closed and open-ended questions;

- A diagram, table, chart, graph, or image about which to answer questions or to analyze; and

- A graphic organizer to complete.

Refer back to the charts in this chapter that identify the different tools available for more specific ideas relevant to your content area.

You can assess student understanding through a variety of means, including the following:

- *Observation:* Set up the interactive whiteboard as a station and monitor student understanding as they complete the activities you have designed individually or in pairs.

- *Oral Response:* More informally, ask students to respond orally to the questions, either individually or in choral response. Listen for the number of correct responses as students respond. Ask students to discuss a question with or explain a process to a partner or small group. Move around the room and listen to the conversations and ask students to share their conclusions with the class.

- *Physical Response:* Ask students to provide a physical response to demonstrate understanding. This can be anything from showing a thumbs up or down to agree or disagree, determine true or false, yes or no, etc. Students can use a shoulder shrug if they do not know. Ask the students what signals their class would like to use to show understanding.

- *Visual Response:* Ask students to hold up an item or card that represents their response to a question. A red card might represent a negative answer, yellow an undecided or unsure answer, and green a positive answer or answer of agreement. Depending on the age and ability level you teach, different things will be appropriate. Ask the students for their thoughts and make sure it is a system you are likely to use as well.

♦ *Written Response:* Ask students to respond to questions on paper if you would like to collect it for later use or if you have a series of questions as part of an exit survey. Pose the questions in written form on the interactive whiteboard. Another way to immediately assess student understanding is through the use of dry erase boards. Ask students to create a response to a question or image you have on the interactive whiteboard and to hold up their answer for you. This is powerful because not only can you see what they are thinking right away, you can also provide the students with immediate feedback. You can also ask students to draw a response to a question you pose. Ask another student volunteer to write or draw their responses on the interactive whiteboard if that works in your classroom.

♦ *Live Poll Response:* If you have access to laptops or another mobile device like a cell phone with texting or an iPod Touch with Internet access, you can make use of them to formatively assess students. Student responses will show in real time on the interactive whiteboard when you use a live polling website. Use the results to stimulate a discussion, see what students are understanding in the middle of the lesson so you can continue or make appropriate adjustments, find out where students are at the end of a class period so you can plan for the next class, etc. A search for *live audience poll* will help you find different sites that offer the service. The services listed offer a basic free account to get started and most will allow students to respond by sending a text message or through a mobile web-based device or a laptop using the Internet. Here are a couple you can check out to get started:

- http://www.polleverywhere.com/
- http://www.smspoll.net/

♦ *Response Systems:* Companies that produce interactive whiteboards also offer their own response systems that sync with their software. Questions can be created in the interactive whiteboard software to assess student understanding. SMART Technologies, at the time of the writing of this book, offers five different options for response tools.

Conclusion

There are many tools and resources available in the Notebook to help you create engaging and interactive lessons. Take your time to explore them as many of the tools have multiple uses. Avoid thinking that you have to master all of the tools at once; instead, start with the ones that you think you will get the most regular use out of for your subject area and the ones that your students are likely to find the most engaging. In time, you will have developed your own collection of highly effective and interesting tools that you are comfortable using.

6

Students Examine
and Create

Idea 9: Students Examine Work

Examine and Interact with Models of Quality Work

An important part of the learning process is for student to examine models of quality work from their peers and professionals. The interactive whiteboard offers many tools that allow students to study the work of others in a more engaging way. While the example that follows looks specifically at models of writing, the different tools available can be used to examine anything from processes in solving math equations to elements of a painting. Both the students and teacher can use the tools to focus on particular elements of what they are examining. Providing students with models, both good and not so good, allows students to think critically and engage in discussion to determine what quality looks like, and then strive to apply it to their own work.

Useful Tools for Examining Models

The Notebook software provides many tools that allow students to examine work in an interactive way. Chapter 1 identified where to find and how to use the different colored Pen, Highlighter, Spotlight, and Magnifier tools. You can also use the Line tool to underline, in addition to the Pen tool. For a writing class, open any type of writing sample that you would like to examine with students. It is helpful for students to also have their own copy of that sample in front of them. Ask students at their seats look for any number of things, including:

- Parts of speech
- Compound sentences
- Hyperbole
- Transition words
- Detail-rich sentences

- Introductory sentences
- Characteristics of main characters
- Rhyming words

The list of what students can look for is endless. Depending upon what you teach and the grade level, you may ask students to identify the desired element on their paper individually or in small groups. You can also model the desired outcome with the interactive whiteboard by asking students as a class to identify examples of what they should be looking for. Involve students by asking them to highlight an example of a detail-rich sentence and identify a reason why it is on the interactive whiteboard. Students not at the board can do this on their own sheets. Another student can circle a transition word with the blue Pen and underline two rhyming words with green Pens or the Line tool on the whiteboard. Use the Spotlight tool or Magnifier to focus in on a specific word, sentence or part of a sentence. As a class you can come up with the tools and color codes to use for different parts of speech and different elements of a good paragraph or story.

Use the different color tools for math problems and equations as well. Consistently use one color Pen to write the plus sign in addition problems and a different color for minus problems if you find students are not paying attention to which sign is which. For algebraic equations, try representing the x variable in one color and the y variable in another to make them stand out. Ask students to explain the process that they used to solve an equation by circling or highlighting key steps. Use the Highlighter tool to highlight the side(s) or angle(s) of a triangle that you want students to focus on when identifying different types of triangles. Ask students to use the tools as well when they show steps and explain their thought processes to the class.

The color Pen tools, Magnifier, and Spotlight are helpful for getting students to focus on a particular element. Students should also become comfortable using those tools to identify important points in explaining their own thinking processes as they examine the work of others, as well as their own.

Idea 10: Students Present their Learning

The interactive whiteboard can play an important role in giving students an opportunity to help design the criteria by which they will be assessed, and once they have created their work, to present it to the class.

Students as Part of the Assessment Design Process

Traditionally, how students will be assessed and what they will be assessed on has been determined solely by teachers. However, as learning shifts in the twenty-first century, learners are increasingly being included in this process. Including the learners in the process helps them better understand and articulate what it is that they need to know and demonstrate. Although taking the first steps toward this shift is uncomfortable, it can be very valuable for both students and teachers, as it creates more of a partnership. The more students and teachers can converse about learning, the greater this partnership can become. The more I have discussed the learning process with students, the more they have become invested in the process because they have a better sense of why they are doing what they are doing. What is also interesting is that they often come up with the same or similar criteria that the teacher does, but because they are involved in the generation process, they better understand the goals and purposes of what they are doing.

You can use the interactive whiteboard as a way to capture students' ideas about what they should be assessed on and how they should be assessed about it. As an example, for creating a blog writing rubric for an introductory level Spanish class, begin by asking students to discuss in small groups what traits make for good writing and how their writing should be assessed. The following are some questions you might give students to discuss:

- What are characteristics of good writing in Spanish I? (List at least six characteristics.)

- Who should evaluate your blogs? (self, other students, teacher, students from other classes, parents, professionals, etc.)

- What type of feedback would you like about your blogs?

- How should they be scored?

- How will you know that your writing is improving?

Once students have had sufficient time to discuss and write down their ideas, bring the group back together and have the groups share their responses. Write down those ideas on the interactive whiteboard and take part in the student discussion, guiding and asking questions as needed. Repeat the process with as many classes as you have at that level. Take what the students came up with in the different classes share the results among all your classes and then create some general categories for the rubric. Figure 6.1 (page 138) is a rubric outline that resulted from the discussions my students had about their writing.

Figure 6.1. Student-Generated Rubric Categories

		Proficient	
Organization			
Content and Ideas			
Sentence Structure			
Sentence Quality			
Spelling and Punctuation			

If necessary add anything you believe is missing and then share the rubric outline with the class to see if the students are in agreement. In most cases, they are likely to agree with what has been generated. If not, make any reasonable adjustments to the categories.

The next step is for students to define what quality writing looks like for each of the categories they have previously determined. Provide students with the rubric that only contains the categories and ask them to once again, in groups, discuss and determine the traits of quality writing for each category. Once they have had time to discuss and write down their results, come back together again as a group and have students share. Use the interactive whiteboard to process and record the findings of the different groups from the different classes. If it seems that there is anything important the students might have missed, ask guiding questions to help them discover it.

The last step is for you to compile the class results into the rubric, keeping the language in student-friendly terms and then re-present the rubric to the students for final approval. It does take more class time to go through this process with the students, but in the end they are more invested and have a better understanding of what type of writing they need to be working toward achieving. The students can also better articulate in self-reflections where they are at in the process of developing their writing and can identify areas in which they still need to work. The interactive whiteboard allows you to easily collect the ideas of the different classes and save them to share with other classes. It also provides you will a record of those conversations to which you and the students can refer back.

Although this is a relatively simple use of the tool, it is collaborative and the outcome can be very powerful. Figure 6.2 is a sample student-generated rubric. The columns on either side of the Proficient classification are for comments from the teacher with suggestions for improvement or identification of advanced traits.

Figure 6.2. Sample Student-Created Rubric

Writing Qualities		Proficient	
Organization		♦ The paragraphs are organized in a clear order.	
Ideas and Content		♦ The ideas make sense and are on topic. ♦ Many adjectives are used. ♦ The questions who, what, when, where, why, how, how much, etc., are answered in the paragraph to provide detail.	
Sentence Structure		85% of the time or more: ♦ The correct article (un, una, unos, unas or el, la, los, las) is used. ♦ The verbs are conjugated correctly. ♦ The adjectives come after the noun. ♦ The nouns and adjectives agree in gender and number.	
Sentence Quality		♦ Sentences are descriptive. ♦ Connecting and transition words are used frequently. ♦ Most sentences are compound. Some may be simpler.	
Spelling and Punctuation		♦ There are minimal accent, spelling, and punctuation errors.	

Students Present Their Work to an Audience

The interactive whiteboard is a helpful tool for getting students involved in the initial stages of assessment design. It is also a great tool for having students present their work to an audience. As part of the twenty-first century shift in instruction and learning, teachers are moving away from having students just turn in work for teacher assessment only. Students tend to be more motivated about the projects and products they are creating when they know there is an audience beyond the teacher and when they have some choice in the tool that they use to demonstrate their understanding. This part of the chapter provides an overview of a few tools that will allow students to creatively demonstrate the learning objectives upon which you, or you and your students collaboratively, have decided. The interactive whiteboard becomes a tool that lets students demonstrate what they have learned to an audience in their classroom. With tools like Skype and video-conferencing software, that audience can extend beyond the walls of the classroom to include local audiences such as parents, grandparents, students in other classrooms across town, experts at local businesses, and similar audiences across the globe.

Types of Presentations

The tools annotated below are just a small selection of what is currently available for students to use to demonstrate their learning. They are organized by the type of project to which the tool lends itself. You may find that some of the tools will be resilient and improve over time to keep up with new advancements, whereas others may be replaced by a newer resource. The annotated lists below are not meant to be exhaustive, but to give ideas about what types of tools students can use to present their work. Depending upon where your school and students are in the technology integration and transformation process, you will approach the use of the tools differently. As much as possible, try to have students select the tool that will work the best for them. There are excellent sources of information about new technology tools for education compiled by educators dedicated to improving student learning. Try to follow one or more of those educators who have invested time in keeping others updated on those tools through blogs, websites, Twitter, etc. The list below includes links to free software and web resources that students can use to demonstrate and share their learning.

Writing Presentations

- ◆ Word processing software

Depending upon the assignment or project, basic word processing documents and spreadsheets software can help students demonstrate part or all of an objective.

♦ Blogging websites

There are many different blogging options. Blogs allow students to track writing progress and idea development over time. They also lend themselves well to helping students reflect about their work. Here are a few to check out.

- http://kidblog.org/home.php

  Blog site with a friendly interface for K-12 bloggers that offers a private and public sharing option for the blogs. This site also allows audio and video to be embedded as part of the students' blogs. Students and teachers can respond to one another's blogs. Teacher's comments can be shared privately with the blog creator or shared publicly with the class.

- http://www.classchatter.com/

  Blog site that allows safe and secure blog posting for class members only. It has a variety of features for how the blogs can be set up.

- http://edublogs.org/

  Blog site for educational use with multiple options for users.

♦ Wiki creation sites

Students can work collaboratively on projects as a class or in smaller groups using a wiki. They can use their wiki as a means to share what they have created with the class. Here are a few wiki hosting sites to check out.

- *PB Works:* http://pbworks.com/

  Students collaboratively create and share content and projects.

- *Wiki Dot:* http://www.wikidot.com/

  Students collaboratively create and share content and projects.

- *Notemesh.com:* http://notemesh.com/?a=home

This wiki allows students to share class notes with one another, giving students access to better information to put projects together.

- ◆ Other writing options
  - • *Tagxedo:* http://www.tagxedo.com/

    Create word shapes with your own words or through various other search options. Similar to Wordle, but with more advanced features.

  - • *Wordle:* http://www.wordle.net/

    Create word clouds with key concepts or vocabulary words from any context.

  - • *Word it Out:* http://worditout.com/

    This site also allows the creation of word clouds with some different settings.

Voice Presentations

There are many accessible resources for voice recording that enable students to create simple voice recordings to add into other presentations, songs and podcasts.

- ◆ *Audacity:* http://audacity.sourceforge.net/

  Create voice recordings with effects, songs, and voice-only podcasts. Make sure to also down the LAME encoder to be able to convert files to an MP3 format.

- ◆ *GarageBand:* GarageBand is software available on the Macintosh that allows students to record voice and real instruments, create music with the recorded rhythms and instruments that are part of the software, and also create visual podcasts.

- ◆ *Voki:* http://www.voki.com/

  Design an avatar and add your voice to it with a computer microphone, the text-to-speech tool, or by recording your voice on the phone.

- ◆ *Vocaroo:* http://www.vocaroo.com/

  With this site and a computer microphone, easily record your voice to embed the audio into a blog, website, or presentation.

- ◆ *Skype:* http://www.skype.com

Record a conversation, interview, discussion, or debate with another student or professional in the field—locally or globally.

Videos

There are a variety of ways students can create videos. They can record themselves acting out scenes, narrate a photo slideshow, create an animated video, and more. Here are a few resources students might try for video project creation.

- *iMovie:* This software is available on the Macintosh and allows students to record and edit their video. Students can create the video by adding pictures and recorded sounds from other sources. Students can also add in subtitles to their work.

- *Windows Movie Maker:* This software is free for computers using Windows and comes installed on newer computers. It allows you to record and edit movies, add transitions and effects, and add music and narration.

- *Masher:* http://www.masher.com/

  Create a video using photos, video clips, and music tracks.

- *Stupeflix:* http://www.stupeflix.com/

  Produce a video with text, images, and music.

- *Animoto:* http://animoto.com/

  Make a video using text, images, and music.

- *PhotoPeach:* http://photopeach.com/

  Create an audiovisual slide show with images and captions.

- *http://memoov.com/*

  Produce animated movies with audio narration.

Screencasting

Students can create an explanation of a process using screencasting tools. Screencasting tools allow a student to show what is on their computer screen and provide a demonstration or explanation of a process with or without audio and text.

- *Jing:* http://www.jingproject.com/

  Capture a shot of what is on your screen or record and explain a process with this tool.

♦ *Cam Studio:* http://camstudio.org/

Record screen and audio activity to create a video and add screen captions with text.

♦ *Wink:* http://www.debugmode.com/wink/

Create screen captures, record a video of your screen with audio, and add explanation boxes and buttons.

Multimedia Presentations

♦ Presentational software

These software programs still have a place for students when preparing informational presentations. Depending upon the program, it will offer the flexibility to include text, images, sounds, animations and videos to create a multimedia presentation. You can use programs that you have available on your school computers like PowerPoint, Keynote, or SMART Notebook, as well as online creation tools.

♦ Online Presentational Tools

• *Kerpoof:* http://www.kerpoof.com/

Create a scene with different backgrounds and images. Create the text for the scene with text boxes and speech bubbles. Kerpoof also allows students to create videos.

• *Glogster Edu:* http://edu.glogster.com/

Create interactive online posters that allow users to include images, clip art, hyperlinks, video, sound, and text.

• *Voice Thread:* http://voicethread.com/

Create presentations with images, documents, and video that the creator can narrate or ask questions about and others can respond to with text or audio.

Review Games

Students can use existing resources on the web to allow them to create games to review important information from class.

♦ *What 2 Learn:* http://www.what2learn.com/

Use their Flash-based interactive game templates to create your own review game or create your own.

♦ *Super Teacher Tools:* http://www.superteachertools.com/

Use the Flash-based interactive game templates to create review games.

Evaluating Presentations

Once students have created a project to share, they can present their projects to their classmates and teacher or to other invited guests using the interactive whiteboard. Invited guests can be present in person or connect with the class and view the presentations using a tool like Skype or other video conferencing software. Skype has a screen-sharing option that allows the presenter to show what is on their computer screen to the person with whom they are Skyping. Students can use the touch sensitivity of interactive whiteboard and its other tools to interact with their presentations and invite the audience to as well.

The audience plays an important role in that they give the students a real group of people to whom they can present and from whom they can receive feedback about the quality of their work. The audience can provide feedback to the presenters in various formats, depending upon the access to technological resources and the age and ability levels of the audience.

Students can also interact with one another with virtual comments. Course managers like Moodle provide forums where students can post their work to share with their classmates and receive feedback from them. Social networking spaces like Edmodo (http://www.edmodo.com/) also allow students to upload their work for peer and teacher feedback. I have found that my students particularly enjoy being able to read the feedback their peers leave in social networking and forum spaces. Students will need time to practice their feedback skills and at first need more of a guide as to what is appropriate and constructive feedback. Peer and teacher feedback help students reflect on the quality of their work and if combined with a self-reflection completed by the individual or team who created the project, can be even more meaningful for the student. Students can reflect on many different parts of the presentation including the process involved to create it to the product they made. If students have been involved in the project and rubric design, that should improve their understanding of the objectives and help them better articulate a self-evaluation.

Students in the audience will also benefit from being able to see and comment on the work of their peers to get ideas on how to improve their own work in the future. Presenting on the big screen of the interactive whiteboard offers students a way to share with an audience of peers and other invited guests and can help students build confidence to share their work globally through outlets like SchoolTube, TeacherTube, and other sharing sites.

Conclusion

Teachers and students can use the interactive whiteboard to display and assess models of student and professional work. The tools available with the software allow users to focus in on key elements of the work with spotlights, highlighters, pens, and shape tools to better evaluate the models. The class discussions can be recorded and saved for later use. Based on evaluation of models, teachers can guide students as they determine the criteria and design rubrics for proficient work. The interactive whiteboard also offers students a medium through which they can share their understanding of what they have learned through multimedia presentations with both local and global audiences.

Conclusion

Variety is important when creating interactive whiteboard lessons if you want students to be engaged and reach deeper levels of understanding of the material. The following are questions to remember as you begin the process of putting together your interactive whiteboard lessons.

- ♦ What kind of questions are you asking? Will they encourage further exploration and inquiry about the topic?

- ♦ What hide-and-reveal tools are you using to add interactivity and to present questions and reveal answers in the lesson? Are you using a variety of them?

- ♦ What types of multimedia experiences are you including with the lesson? Do the images and video clips help students better visualize and understand the concept? Are the videos just long enough or too long? Is there a good mixture of quality questions and discussion to accompany the video clips?

- ♦ What types of interactive resources are you or the students finding online to enrich the lesson and deepen students' understanding? How are students engaging with the resources—as a whole class, in small groups, individually?

- ♦ What types of resources are you finding in the Lesson Activity Toolkit to help make the material that you are previewing, presenting, practicing or reviewing more interactive for the students?

- ♦ What other tools are you finding in the Notebook software to help students process and synthesize information?

- ♦ How are you using the interactive whiteboard to help you assess students' progress?

- ♦ How are students using the board to demonstrate their learning to you and others? How are students reflecting on their work after they have shared it with their audience?

Speaking from my own experiences in learning how to use the interactive whiteboard, it is a journey and a process. Having asked myself the previous questions helped me reflect on and improve my own lessons. The first lessons I created were not always my best ones. Creating lessons with the interactive whiteboard can be paralleled a bit to the revision process when writing. The first draft is rarely the best, but with suggestions from and discussions with peers and experts and the ability to reflect and be critical of one's own work, the drafts improve. I saw my lessons differently the second time around in a way that I could not have seen the first time, as much as I really would have liked to. At times that was frustrating because it meant I needed to revise them, but because of that critical reflection process, students benefited from better lessons and instruction. Remember that any time you learn anything new involves a substantial investment of time, energy, and resources, but it is well worth the journey. Be patient with yourself and have fun with it!

References and Resources

Books

Betcher, Chris, and Mal Lee. (2009). *The Interactive Whiteboard Revolution.* Camberwell, Victoria, AU: Acer Press.

Reeves, Douglas, ed. (2007). *Ahead of the Curve: The Power of Assessment to Transform Teaching and Learning.* Bloomington, IN: Solution Tree Press.

Wagner, Tony. (2008). *The Global Achievement Gap.* New York, NY: Basic Books.

Training Manuals

SMART Technologies ULC. (2008). *Notebook Software Training for SMART Board: Level 1 Facilitator's Guide.* Calgary, Alberta, Canada.

SMART Technologies ULC. (2008). *Notebook Software Training for SMART Board: Level 2 Facilitator's Guide.* Calgary, Alberta, Canada.

Web Resources

http://www.smarttech.com

Downloads and software updates for SMART Notebook software

http://smarttech.com/trainingcenter/material.asp

Check out the different areas for support, especially the one entitled *SMART Notebook Software 10* for training handouts and videos.

http://www2.smarttech.com/kbdoc/131883

This reference explains the differences between what is supported in the Notebook software with different operating systems: Windows, Mac, and Linux.

http://downloads01.smarttech.com/media/trainingcenter/nb_basics_learning_resource.pdf

This 38-page resource has many helpful tips for using your SMART Board.

http://exchange.smarttech.com/index.html

This is a source of SMART Board lessons that teachers share.

http://www.teacherslovesmartboards.com

  SMART Board tips, resources and podcasts

http://www.freetech4teachers.com/

  General technology resource site that includes resources for interactive whiteboards.

http://iwbrevolution.ning.com/

  Educators sharing ideas, lessons, and video clips about using the interactive whiteboard.

http://docs.google.com/present/view?id=dhn2vcv5_106c9fm8j

  Interesting ways to use the interactive whiteboard in the classroom.

http://foi.becta.org.uk/content_files/corporate/resources/foi/archived_publications/getting_most_whiteboard_secondary.pdf

  Getting the Most from Your Interactive Whiteboard publication from the British Educational Communications and Technology Agency.

http://publications.becta.org.uk/display.cfm?resID=25918

  Teaching Interactively with Electronic Whiteboards in the Primary Phase publication from the British Educational Communications and Technology Agency.

http://www2.smarttech.com/NR/rdonlyres/2C729F6E-0A8D-42B8-9B32-F90BE0A746D8/0/Int_Whiteboard_Research_Whitepaper_Update.pdf

  Interactive Whiteboards and Learning: Improving Student Learning Outcomes and Streamlining Lesson Planning publication from SMART Technologies.

http://downloads01.smarttech.com/media/research/international_research/uk/becta_researchreport.pdf

  Research Bulletin: Interactive Whiteboards Significantly Affect Teaching and Learning publication from SMART Technologies.

http://homepage.mac.com/gwashburne/FileSharing2.html

  This site offers hands on practice activities and explanations in Notebook, as well as game templates from SMART Technologies.

http://edorigami.wikispaces.com/file/view/bloom%27s+Digital+taxonomy+v3.01.pdf

  Ways to apply Bloom's Digital Taxonomy.

Video Tutorials

http://www.youtube.com

Check out the tutorial videos for using Notebook software on You-Tube. Try a search like *SMART Board tutorials* along with the topic you are looking to learn about.

http://www.youtube.com/user/SMARTClassrooms

SMART Classroom's YouTube Videos offer video tutorials on numerous topics.

http://smarttech.com/trainingcenter/

SMART offers various video tutorials from its online training center resource.

Web Resources for Using Notebook 10 with a Macintosh

http://downloads.smarttech.com/media/sitecore/en/support/Product/SmartNotebook/SMARTNotebookSoftware10Windows/Other/OS-ComparisonSMARTNotebook10v01Sept09.pdf

Comparison SMART Notebook Software 10: Microsoft Windows, Mac OS, and Linux Operating Systems from SMART Technologies.

http://www.smarttech.com/us/Support/Browse+Support/Product+Index/Software+Products/SMART+Notebook/Version+10+for+Mac

This link takes you to the most current product information for using Notebook 10 with the Macintosh. You can also get there by going to http://www.smarttech.com and clicking on Browse Support. From there select Notebook 10 as the product and then pick the Macintosh version.

http://downloads.smarttech.com/media/sitecore/en/support/Product/SmartNotebook/SMARTNotebookSoftware10Mac/Guides/Guide-Note10Macv15Apr09.pdf

How to create Notebook files for the Mac OS.

Piedmont College Libraries

10128920